INTRODUCING
ISSUES WITH
OPPOSING
VIEWPOINTS®

Video
Games

Jill Hamilton, *Book Editor*

GREENHAVEN PRESS
A part of Gale, Cengage Learning

GALE
CENGAGE Learning

Detroit • New York • San Francisco • New Haven, Conn • Waterville, Maine • London

Christine Nasso, *Publisher*
Elizabeth Des Chenes, *Managing Editor*

© 2011 Greenhaven Press, a part of Gale, Cengage Learning

For more information, contact:
Greenhaven Press
27500 Drake Rd.
Farmington Hills, MI 48331-3535
Or you can visit our Internet site at gale.cengage.com

For product information and technology assistance, contact us at

Gale Customer Support, 1-800-877-4253
For permission to use material from this text or product, submit all requests online at
www.cengage.com/permissions

Further permissions questions can be e-mailed to permissionrequest@cengage.com

Articles in Greenhaven Press anthologies are often edited for length to meet page require-ments. In addition, original titles of these works are changed to clearly present the main thesis and to explicitly indicate the author's opinion. Every effort is made to ensure that Greenhaven Press accurately reflects the original intent of the authors. Every effort has been made to trace the owners of copyrighted material.

Cover image copyright © Jupiterimages/Comstock/Getty Images.

LIBRARY OF CONGRESS CATALOGING-IN-PUBLICATION DATA

Video games / Jill Hamilton, Book Editor.
    p. cm. -- (Introducing issues with opposing viewpoints)
  Includes bibliographical references and index.
  ISBN 978-0-7377-4946-5 (hardcover)
  1. Video games--Psychological aspects. 2. Computer games--Psychological aspects.
3. Learning, Psychology of. 4. Learning--Social aspects. I. Hamilton, Jill.
  GV1469.3.V5258 2010
  793.93'2--dc22
                                                                        2010018198

Printed in the United States of America
1 2 3 4 5 6 7 14 13 12 11 10

Contents

Chapter 3: Do Video Games Portray Minorities Fairly?

Foreword

Indulging in a wide spectrum of ideas, beliefs, and perspectives is a critical cornerstone of democracy. After all, it is often debates over differences of opinion, such as whether to legalize abortion, how to treat prisoners, or when to enact the death penalty, that shape our society and drive it forward. Such diversity of thought is frequently regarded as the hallmark of a healthy and civilized culture. As the Reverend Clifford Schutjer of the First Congregational Church in Mansfield, Ohio, declared in a 2001 sermon, "Surrounding oneself with only like-minded people, restricting what we listen to or read only to what we find agreeable is irresponsible. Refusing to entertain doubts once we make up our minds is a subtle but deadly form of arrogance." With this advice in mind, Introducing Issues with Opposing Viewpoints books aim to open readers' minds to the critically divergent views that comprise our world's most important debates.

Introducing Issues with Opposing Viewpoints simplifies for students the enormous and often overwhelming mass of material now available via print and electronic media. Collected in every volume is an array of opinions that captures the essence of a particular controversy or topic. Introducing Issues with Opposing Viewpoints books embody the spirit of nineteenth-century journalist Charles A. Dana's axiom: "Fight for your opinions, but do not believe that they contain the whole truth, or the only truth." Absorbing such contrasting opinions teaches students to analyze the strength of an argument and compare it to its opposition. From this process readers can inform and strengthen their own opinions, or be exposed to new information that will change their minds. Introducing Issues with Opposing Viewpoints is a mosaic of different voices. The authors are statesmen, pundits, academics, journalists, corporations, and ordinary people who have felt compelled to share their experiences and ideas in a public forum. Their words have been collected from newspapers, journals, books, speeches, interviews, and the Internet, the fastest growing body of opinionated material in the world.

Introducing Issues with Opposing Viewpoints shares many of the well-known features of its critically acclaimed parent series, Opposing Viewpoints. The articles are presented in a pro/con format, allowing readers to absorb divergent perspectives side by side. Active reading questions preface each viewpoint, requiring the student to approach the material thoughtfully and carefully. Useful charts, graphs, and cartoons supplement each article. A thorough introduction provides readers with crucial background on an issue. An annotated bibliography points the reader toward articles, books, and Web sites that contain additional information on the topic. An appendix of organizations to contact contains a wide variety of charities, nonprofit organizations, political groups, and private enterprises that each hold a position on the issue at hand. Finally, a comprehensive index allows readers to locate content quickly and efficiently.

Introducing Issues with Opposing Viewpoints is also significantly different from Opposing Viewpoints. As the series title implies, its presentation will help introduce students to the concept of opposing viewpoints and learn to use this material to aid in critical writing and debate. The series' four-color, accessible format makes the books attractive and inviting to readers of all levels. In addition, each viewpoint has been carefully edited to maximize a reader's understanding of the content. Short but thorough viewpoints capture the essence of an argument. A substantial, thought-provoking essay question placed at the end of each viewpoint asks the student to further investigate the issues raised in the viewpoint, compare and contrast two authors' arguments, or consider how one might go about forming an opinion on the topic at hand. Each viewpoint contains sidebars that include at-a-glance information and handy statistics. A Facts About section located in the back of the book further supplies students with relevant facts and figures.

Following in the tradition of the Opposing Viewpoints series, Greenhaven Press continues to provide readers with invaluable exposure to the controversial issues that shape our world. As John Stuart Mill once wrote: "The only way in which a human being can make some approach to knowing the whole of a subject is by hearing what can be said about it by persons of every variety of opinion and studying all modes in which it can be looked at by every character of mind. No wise man ever acquired his wisdom in any mode but this." It is to this principle that Introducing Issues with Opposing Viewpoints books are dedicated.

Introduction

"Games are just evolving like species in order to fit into every little niche of our lives."

—Jesse Schell, Carnegie Mellon University
instructor of entertainment technology,
National Public Radio, March 8, 2010

In their short history, video games have gone from futuristic novelty to, for many, a ubiquitous part of modern life. The value of video games and the roles games should have in the lives of gamers is still being debated, but one thing is certain, video games are becoming more entrenched in daily activities. In 2009 Americans spent nearly $20 billion on video game equipment, according to the NPD Group, a market research firm. This was double the amount spent on video gaming five years before. Games even played a role in presidential politics when, during the 2008 election, then-candidate Barack Obama placed ads in several online sports games, including *Madden NFL 09.*

Video games had quite modest beginnings. Sixty years ago it would have been difficult to imagine how prevalent they would become. One of the earliest games was developed simply to entertain guests on visitor's day at a science lab. In 1958 scientist Willy Higinbotham was looking for something to entertain visitors to Brookhaven National Laboratory in Upton, New York. "It might liven up the place to have a game that people could play, and which could convey the message that our scientific endeavors have relevance for society," he wrote later, according to the *New York Times* on November 7, 2008. He came up with a primitive *Pong*-like game called *Tennis for Two,* which was played on an oscilloscope and controlled by knobs and buttons. Although the game was certainly popular on visitor's day, it did not create much stir beyond the lab.

Video games did not arrive in American homes until almost twenty years later with the advent of the first home video game system, Magnavox's Odyssey, and later Atari's *Pong* game. When *Pong* was first released in 1975, it was sold only in Sears stores but quickly became the hottest present of the year. Two years later Atari introduced its

When Atari's game Pong *came out in 1975, it quickly became the must-have item of the year.*

cartridge video game system Atari 2600. Around the same time, video games were becoming popular in arcades as well. The popular *Space Invaders* came out in 1978 and *Pac-Man* in 1980. As in-home game systems became increasingly sophisticated, more people tried gaming. Blockbuster games like the Halo series, first introduced in 2001, and Nintendo's popular Wii system, launched in 2006, helped bring video games to an even wider audience.

In the earliest days of video game history, games were mostly popular with teenage boys. Today that stereotype of a typical gamer persists, though statistics show that it is no longer true. Boys aged seventeen or younger make up only 18 percent of gamers according to the Entertainment Software Association (ESA). Women make up 40 percent of gamers, and 25 percent of people older than fifty play video games. The average age of the most frequent game purchaser is thirty-five, according to the ESA.

As more people are playing, video games have become a big business. *Call of Duty: Modern Warfare 2*, the best-selling game of 2009, sold 11.86 million copies. With sales and profits close to those in the moviemaking business, companies are willing to spend more on video games. In 2010 a top game could take more than three years to make and cost more than $100 million, according to Joshua Brockman on National Public Radio. The gaming industry creates jobs in a variety of fields like game design, programming, and art and animation. There are about forty-five thousand jobs in the industry, with an average salary of about eighty thousand dollars, according to Game Developer Research. These numbers are expected to increase.

In addition, video games are no longer just for play. Games are used for a variety of purposes in schools, from *Dance Dance Revolution* in gym class to *Sim City* for budding engineers. Businesses also are using games for recruiting and training. Employee training at the Hilton Garden Inn includes *Ultimate Team Play*, a virtual reality game in which trainees have to decide the best way to respond to guest demands, according to the game's maker, Virtual Heroes, Inc. Games are used to teach firefighters and police officers how to respond to terrorists attacks, railroad employees how to move train cars safely, and technicians how to repair copy machines.

Games are also being used for therapeutic purposes. They have been used for treating phobias, helping physical therapy patients improve their range of motion, and as a distraction from pain. Therapists at

A stroke victim uses the Wii Sports Boxing *game as part of his physical therapy program.*

the Walter Reed Army Medical Center use a game called *Virtual Iraq* as part of the treatment for soldiers suffering from post-traumatic stress disorder.

Games are increasingly available in more places and through more media. Many people have near-constant access to games through cell phones, iPods, or portable game systems like PSP or Nintendo DS. Likewise, anyone with an Internet connection is just a click or two away from a vast array of online games. Video games are available in hospitals, on airplanes, and in cars. In the future experts predict that games will become further entrenched in daily living. In the works are games that can be played with no controller, games that offer frequent player rewards, games that can be ordered on demand, and in-store games like treasure hunts or other missions offered by retailers to entice customers.

In *Introducing Issues with Opposing Viewpoints: Video Games*, the authors offer their views on the major issues surrounding video games today, including whether video game violence is harmful, how games should be used in education, and whether some games should be banned. As games become even more prevalent in homes, schools, and workplaces, the decisions about the role of games in the lives of gamers and others will become more important than ever.

Chapter 1

Do Video Games Have a Positive Impact on Society?

Video games can be a means for families to spend quality time together, but they can also lead to problems.

Video Games Offer Users a Rich Experience

Naomi Alderman

"Computer games can be works of art and literature; . . . the real neglect would be to deny our children the opportunity to understand and enjoy them."

In the following selection Naomi Alderman argues that video games can be forms of art and literature. As in art and literature, she writes, there are sometimes violent themes, but these can provide a starting point for important conversations between parents and children about the world. She also writes that too much attention is paid to portraying games as "psychotic killing sprees" when, in reality, many games are beautiful, moving, and inspiring. Alderman is a British writer and game designer.

AS YOU READ, CONSIDER THE FOLLOWING QUESTIONS:

1. The author compares being "addicted" to a video game to being "engrossed" in a what?
2. Alderman notes a positive mission in *Grand Theft Auto 3.* What is it?
3. The author recommends several video games, calling them "enchanting." Name two of them.

On [April 8, 2008] the Advertising Standards Agency banned adverts [British term for advertisements] for a new computer game, *Kane & Lynch*, because it deemed them too violent. It is interesting that adverts for last year's "torture porn" film *Captivity* were not banned, even though they were heavily criticised in the US. And no one even raises the possibility of banning such films outright. But then, computer games are our society's straw man [a front man used to divert attention from the real issue] for panic about moral decay, thought to have some special power to harm and corrupt.

Dr Tanya Byron's eminently sensible report last month [March 2008] on children and new technology emphasised the many opportunities for fun and learning that games provide. But the media coverage focused on the usual fears and worries. Byron said that we need to

Top-Selling Games in the United Kingdom

1	*Just Dance*
2	*Call of Duty: Modern Warfare 2*
3	*Wii Fit Plus*
4	*Army of Two: The 40th Day*
5	*Wii Sports Resort*
6	*FIFA 10*
7	*New Super Mario Bros.* Wii
8	*James Cameron's Avatar: The Game*
9	*Assassin's Creed II*
10	*Mario Kart.* Wii

Data is for the week ending January 23, 2010.

Taken from: GFK Chart Track, January 2010.

move away from talking about computer games "causing harm"; in response, TV and newspapers showed stills from games with titles like *Manhunt* and *God of War*. Byron said children need to be "empowered to keep themselves safe"; newspapers said computers and televisions should be kept in communal spaces in the home.

As a gamer, I can't think of anything more annoying for everyone concerned than playing games in a shared living room. Games make noise: they're surely going to irritate other family members who aren't playing or watching. Not to mention the supreme aggravation, as the player, of having someone interrupt you while you're at a crucial stage, just before a save-point, when you want to devote all your attention to the story. Of course, wanting to devote this amount of attention to a computer game probably demonstrates that I'm "addicted". Unlike, say, if I were reading a novel: then my irritation at being interrupted would just show that I was "engrossed".

> # FAST FACT
>
> **Dr. Kawashima's Brain Training,** which features puzzles designed to improve mental fitness, is the United Kingdom's top-selling game of all time.

I'm probably biased. As a child in the 1980s I had both a television and a computer in my bedroom. The computer was a ZX Spectrum 48K, and the best thing it could do was spend 45 minutes trying to load *The Hobbit* text adventure before crashing, but there it was. I watched a lot of television, mostly while doing my homework, and sometimes stayed up late playing on the computer. The only lasting effect seems to have been to provide me with the ability to work with any amount of background noise, including, on one occasion, not noticing that the building opposite was surrounded by screaming fire engines when I was trying to finish a piece of work against a tight deadline.

These days, as well as writing prose fiction, I write online computer games, so I expect I'm biased there, too. But there are so many beautiful, moving, inspiring games—many free online—that I really cannot understand the insistence on portraying all games as psychotic killing sprees.

Games Can Lead to Important Discussions

It is true that in *Grand Theft Auto 3* [GTA3] to take an example that is the subject of repeated concern, the main character, Carl Johnson, shoots other characters, steals cars, and sets up a series of racketeering operations staffed by hoodlums. *GTA3* also contains ambulance missions in which the characters ferry people to hospital; these tend not to get so much attention. The world of *Grand Theft Auto* does contain violence and misogyny; but then, so does *The Godfather*, or *Goodfellas*. So, for that matter, does *The Iliad*. *GTA3* is set in a tough, dangerous world. Johnson is trying to clean up his neighbourhood. But as a dispossessed, orphaned young black man, he has no option but to re-form his neighbourhood gang to do so. The makers of this game, like the makers of any movie about gangland, can stand squarely behind the art they have created and say: this represents reality. If it offends you, don't criticise the art, but take action to improve the world around you.

Clearly, these themes are not suitable for young children. But just as a responsible parent wouldn't hand their child a copy of *American Psycho* or sit them down in front of *Marathon Man* without any

Defenders of violent video games such as Grand Theft Auto *argue that there is no more violence in the game than in* The Iliad, *the classic, ancient epic poem by Homer.*

further discussion or comment, games can and should be part of the ongoing conversation between parents and children about the world. Byron's report suggested "health-warning labels" on computer games, but these would just encourage parents to remain entirely disengaged from the games world, still unaware of what messages their children are picking up. I'm afraid there's only one solution: if your children are playing computer games, you should be playing them too.

Don't worry. The gaming world isn't filled only with violence and depravity. In fact, it's mostly enchanting. If you haven't already spent a little time online playing with the sweetly soothing *Samorost* game, or Eyemaze's whimsical Grow series, or Foon's delightful Hapland, I urge you to do so now. And then share them with your children. Introduce teenagers to the satirical online role-playing game *Kingdom of Loathing*. The game I'm writing at the moment, available at wetell stories.co.uk, is a collaboration between the publishers Penguin and games company Six to Start, and involves popular and literary novelists exploring new ways to tell stories online.

Computer games can be works of art and literature—they're still developing. The stories they can tell, and the experiences they provide, are increasingly sophisticated and glorious. And that, of course, is the point. The world that today's 10-year-olds grow into will offer so many rich experiences via video games: the real neglect would be to deny our children the opportunity to understand and enjoy them.

EVALUATING THE AUTHOR'S ARGUMENTS:

Naomi Alderman has a background in literature and game design. Does this make her argument more persuasive or less so? Why or why not?

Some Video Games Should Be Banned

"If parents and rating systems don't prevent these games from falling into the wrong hands then maybe [banning them is] a step that needs to be taken."

Adam Sorice

In the following article Adam Sorice argues that some video games have such objectionable content that they need to be kept out of the hands of young people. He gives examples of inappropriate content from games like *Manhunt* and the Grand Theft Auto series. If parental monitoring and ratings systems are not effective in keeping these games away from children, Sorice writes, then these games should be banned. Sorice calls himself a "hardcore gamer" and is a frequent contributor to online discussions about issues in gaming.

AS YOU READ, CONSIDER THE FOLLOWING QUESTIONS:
1. What are two of the tasks for players in the Grand Theft Auto series, according to the author?
2. How does a player earn a higher score at the end of a level in the game *Manhunt*, according to Sorice?
3. What game gained attention in 2005 for containing an objectionable secret minigame, according to the author?

In today's society, realism has become a pillar of popular entertainment, with TV programs dealing with tougher issues and darker themes appearing in all forms of media. Unfortunately, this has become a scapegoat for government and annoyed adults to blame the behavior of young people on.

One game developer has been at the centre of the controversy of the explosion of popularity in violent games, Rockstar, the creator of criticized series such as Grand Theft Auto and Manhunt.

The studio, originally based in Dundee, Scotland, has unquestionably produced some of the most criticized games in recent years, most notably being the game *Manhunt*, which was banned from sale in various stores in the UK and Europe, due to its connection with the murder charge of a teenage boy.

Both series encourage players to take on the role of convicts and perform various crimes, including serial murder, theft and prostitution, while evading the law. The Grand Theft Auto series sees you join one of the many gangs roaming fictitious cities based on real-life locations, performing various tasks to try and make your gang the strongest in the city, such as murdering significant members of the Mafia or Triad, or further your own career by working for various criminals in the city.

Heinous Violence

In contrast, the game *Manhunt* puts you into control of James Earl Cash, a Death Row prisoner salvaged by a sadistic businessman only known as the Director, who forces him to roam the streets of Carcer City, brutally murdering members of various gangs to be turned into sickeningly violent films, detailing these heinous acts. The player attains a higher score at the end of the level, depending on the severity of the murders performed. As well as being able to decapitate, dismember or suffocate random enemies, the player can perform "executions", such as electrocuting people at the asylum.

However, *Manhunt* hasn't been Rockstar's only folly when it comes to the public. In 2005, the coding of a PC copy of *Grand Theft Auto: San Andreas*, the most recent edition of the series, was hacked into by a gamer, who discovered a mini game titled "Hot Coffee", which allowed players to perform various sexual acts with in-game women.

Rockstar claimed the mini game, which had been written into the coding of the final version but made supposedly inaccessible before release, had been created completely by players. But when it was discovered that the mini game originated completely from within the game itself, Rockstar and publisher Take-Two came under mass criticism from politicians, the ESRB [Entertainment Software Rating Board] and retailers.

Despite past games causing a media backlash, Rockstar once again tried to push the envelope with their newest game, *Manhunt 2*, creating a game featuring a much darker and disturbing experience, enhanced by the Nintendo Wii's motion sensor controls, allowing players to physically act out their murders.

Rating Organizations Ban *Manhunt 2*

However, rating organizations around the world found [a] flaw in *Manhunt 2*, with the game in a way being banned in the United States and the UK [United Kingdom], as well as the Republic of Ireland, Italy and Switzerland. Similar verdicts are expected from Germany and Australia, who banned the original title, *Manhunt*.

The British Board of Film Classification (BBFC) banned *Manhunt 2* on June 19, 2007, making it the first game to be banned in over a decade, and the first ban ever to be extensively upheld. The BBFC stated that the game had an "unrelenting focus on stalking and brutal slaying" and that "there is sustained and cumulative casual sadism in the way in which these killings are committed, and encouraged, in the game."

> **FAST FACT**
>
> No video game has yet been banned in the United States because of the First Amendment. However, retailers often refuse to sell games rated "Adults Only," and console makers will not license them.

In the United States, *Manhunt 2* was originally given an AO (Adults Only) rating by the Entertainment Software Rating Board (ESRB), which effectively banned the game, due to the fact that neither Sony [n]or Nintendo approved of AO-rated games, nor would retailers stock such a severely rated game, due to lawsuits. However, an edited

Top-Ten Banned Video Games Around the World

Game	Banned in	Reason
Call of Duty: Modern Warfare	Saudi Arabia	Cruelty and violence against Islamic soldiers
Sexy Poker	Australia	Sexual content
Condemned 2: Bloodshot	Germany	Violent content
Grand Theft Auto IV	United Arab Emirates (and others)	Violent content
Dark Sector	Australia	Violent content
Mass Effect	Singapore	Same-sex sexual content
Left 4 Dead 2	Australia	Violent content
Fallout 3	India	Portrayal of two-headed cows
Call of Duty: World at War	Japan	Extreme violence against Japanese soldiers
Alien vs. Predator	Australia	Violent content

Taken from: GamesRadar UK, "Top Ten Banned Video Games," December 5, 2009.

version of the game was given an M (Mature) rating, allowing the game to be bought legally by adults in stores (including supermarkets) across the country.

So the debate returns to violent games. Do they cause young people to act violent? Who's to blame: the kids, the parents or the games developers, such as Rockstar, themselves?

I think everyone is partly to blame in situations such as this. Despite the fact that games such as *Grand Theft Auto* and *Manhunt* are rated certificate 18 in the UK, young people have access to them. I have a copy of *Grand Theft Auto 3* that I used to play and looking back on it, I completely agree that these games need to be kept out of [the] hands of young people.

So, if banning games such as *Manhunt 2* is the only way to stop young people playing these kinds of games, then I'm all for it. It's a decision that has split the industry, but if parents and rating systems don't prevent these games from falling into the wrong hands then maybe it's a step that needs to be taken.

And as for Rockstar, maybe they should think about who can really get their hands on their games before releasing another "adult" experience.

EVALUATING THE AUTHOR'S ARGUMENTS:

Adam Sorice details some of the more objectionable content in a few games. Is this a necessary and important part of his argument, in your opinion? Why or why not?

Video Games Can Have Both Positive and Negative Impacts on Children

Douglas A. Gentile

"Parents should recognize that video games can have powerful effects on children."

In the following selection Douglas A. Gentile argues that video games have both positive and negative effects on children and that parents need to be aware of each. The key to maximizing the positive effects while minimizing the negative, writes Gentile, is for parents to set limits on the time their children spend playing games and to make sure the content of the games is suitable for the child. Gentile is a developmental psychologist and the director of research for the National Institute on Media and the Family.

AS YOU READ, CONSIDER THE FOLLOWING QUESTIONS:
1. About how many hours a week do boys and girls play video games on average, according to the article?
2. List two positive effects of video games mentioned by Gentile.
3. The American Academy of Pediatrics recommends that children not spend more than how many hours in front of any electronic screen, according to the author?

The home video game industry is now over 30 years old. In that time, computer technology has improved at a geometric rate. A high speed elevator now has more computing power than the Apollo spacecraft that landed on the moon. The promise of computers and video games as teachers was clearly recognized in the 1980s when there was a nationwide push to get computers into the classrooms. In the years that have followed, researchers found that educational software and games can indeed have several very positive effects on children's academic skill. Over the same period, video games also moved into children's homes. (I define video games broadly here, as including arcade games, computer games, and home console games such as PlayStation.) Children began playing video games for increasing amounts of time, and the games themselves became more graphically violent over time. Parents, educators, physicians, and researchers began to question what the impact of these changes might be.

Among elementary and middle-school populations, girls play for an average of about 5.5 hours/week and boys average 13 hours/week. Playing games is not limited to adolescent boys. Recently, the *Wall Street Journal* reported that several companies are now designing video game consoles for preschoolers. Preschoolers aged two to five play an average of 28 minutes/day. The amount of time spent playing video games is increasing, but not at the expense of television viewing which has remained stable at about 24 hours/week.

Similar to earlier studies about television, the data about children's video game habits are correlated with risk factors for health and with poorer academic performance. When video game play is analyzed for violent content, additional risk factors are observed for aggressive behavior and desensitization to violence.

Video Games Can Have Positive Effects

Video games are natural teachers. Children find them highly motivating; by virtue of their interactive nature, children are actively engaged with them; they provide repeated practice; and they include rewards for skillful play. These facts make it likely that video games could have large effects, some of which are intended by game designers, and some of which may not be intended.

Video games have been shown to teach children healthy skills for the self-care of asthma and diabetes and have been successful at imparting the attitudes, skills, and behaviors that they were designed to teach. In a study with college students, playing a golf video game improved students' actual control of force when putting, even though the video game gave no bodily feedback on actual putting movement or force. There have even been studies with adults showing that experience with video games is related to better surgical skills. Research also suggests that people can learn iconic, spatial, and visual attention skills from video games.

Games Can Also Have Negative Effects

Given the fact that video games are able to have several positive effects, it should come as no surprise that they also can have negative effects. Research has documented negative effects of video games on children's physical health, including obesity, video-induced seizures, and postural, muscular, and skeletal disorders, such as tendonitis, nerve compression, and carpal tunnel syndrome. However, these effects are not likely to occur for most children. The research to date suggests that parents should be most concerned about two things: the amount of time that children play, and the content of the games that they play.

Simply put, the amount of time spent playing video games has a negative correlation with academic performance. Playing violent games has a positive correlation with antisocial and aggressive behav-

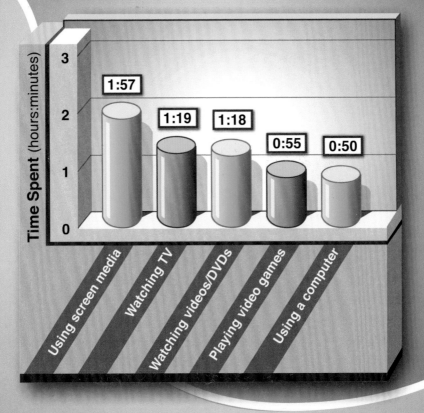

Young Children and Screen Time

Among those who use each medium in a typical day, average amount of time spent by children aged six and under seven.

Time Spent (hours:minutes)

1:57
1:19
1:18
0:55
0:50

Using screen media
Watching TV
Watching videos/DVDs
Playing video games
Using a computer

Taken from: Kaiser Family Foundation, *The Media Family: Electronic Media in the Lives of Infants, Toddlers, Preschoolers, and Their Parents*, May 2006.

ior (most researchers define violence in games as when the player can intentionally harm other characters in the game). Content analyses show that a majority of games contain some violence. A majority of 4th to 8th grade children prefer violent games.

Content Counts

Looking across the dozens of studies that have now been conducted on violent video games, there appear to be five major effects. Playing violent games leads to increased physiological arousal, increased

The American Academy of Pediatrics recommends that children spend no more than fourteen hours per week in front of all types of electronic screens.

aggressive thoughts, increased aggressive feelings, increased aggressive behaviors, and decreased prosocial helping. These studies include experimental studies (where it can be shown that playing violent games actually causes increases in aggression), correlational studies (where long-term relations between game play and real-world aggression can be shown), and longitudinal studies (where changes in children's aggressive behaviors can be demonstrated). For example, in a study of over 400 3rd–5th graders, those students who played more violent video games early in the school year changed to become more physically aggressive later in the school year, even after statistically controlling for sex, race, total screen time, prior aggression, and other relevant variables. Apparently practice does make perfect.

The research also seems to show that parents have an important role to play. Children whose parents limited the amount of time they could play and also used the video game ratings to limit the content of the games have children who do better in school and also get into fewer fights. Regarding limiting the amount, the American Academy of Pediatrics recommends that children not spend more than one to two hours per day in front of all electronic screens, including TV, DVDs, videos, video games (handheld, console, or computer), and computers (for non-academic use). This means seven to fourteen hours per week total. The average school-age child spends over 37 hours a week in front of a screen. We all like to think our children are above average, but on this dimension it's not a good thing. Regarding content, educational games are likely to have positive effects and violent games are likely to have negative effects. Almost all (98%) of pediatricians believe that violent media have a negative effect on children.

The conclusion I draw from the accumulated research is that the question of whether video games are "good" or "bad" for children is oversimplified. Playing a violent game for hours every day could decrease school performance, increase aggressive behaviors, and improve visual attention skills. Instead, parents should recognize that video games can have powerful effects on children, and should therefore set limits on the amount and content of games their children play. In this way, we can realize the potential benefits while minimizing the potential harms.

EVALUATING THE AUTHORS' ARGUMENTS:

Douglas A. Gentile contends that the issue of video game safety is often oversimplified. Do you think the authors of the previous two viewpoints would agree? Explain your answer.

Video Games Can Be the Future of Education

Duncan Fyfe

"Sometimes teaching is like a magic trick. You need to hide the blackboard."

In the following essay Duncan Fyfe argues that video games are the way to create enthusiastic learners. Games, he writes, put students in the right frame of mind to learn. A player deeply involved in a game, he argues, is focused, attentive to detail, and ready to absorb information—exactly the qualities a teacher hopes for in a student. Fyfe is a video game commentator.

AS YOU READ, CONSIDER THE FOLLOWING QUESTIONS:
1. What is an RPG, as described in the article?
2. Mark Twain's technique of drawing readers into arguments on slavery and prejudice through story is the same tactic used in which game, according to Fyfe?
3. *Call of Duty 4* could make gamers more interested in the situation in what region of the world, according to the author?

Duncan Fyfe, "Opinion: Video Games Are the Silver Bullet," GameSetWatch.com, August 8, 2008. Reproduced by permission of the author.

What makes learning fun? Check with any demographic that's high school age or younger and the answer will probably be "nothing."

School is where we are introduced to the idea of learning as a regulated process, and it is expressed to us there as a punitive contract.

Often we try to learn because we fear the consequences, not because—especially not at an early age—we have a Jeffersonian zeal [after Thomas Jefferson] for knowledge. Rare and precocious are the self-made seven-year-old scholars, and the rest become combative and reluctant when faced with calculus and biology.

The truism we learn the best is that learning is work. That's even the case with ostensibly enjoyable subject matter. Kids are smart, and they sense that *To Kill A Mockingbird* is really about writing essays and delivering presentations. Put any great work of literature in a class of high school boys and watch it be diminished to a laughable, pretentious relic. Few can appreciate a classic in that environment.

The problem isn't with the novel or even with the intelligence of the boys. The contract of learning is the problem. In high school, they'll discover way more about chlamydia than they will about [the poet John] Keats. Students are conditioned to approach literature with entirely the wrong mindset.

Allow Learning to Entertain

The trick to enthusiastic learning is the trick. We need to have the right attitude, need to be in the right frame of mind to develop interests in art on its own terms and at our own pace. It's not necessary to instantly attempt a codification [a system of standards] of its merits even when the art does not move us to speak.

We grow up viewing classic fiction as homework first and art second. It follows that we like learning best when we don't think we're doing it. We like literature more when there's no studying involved. What better medium for learning, then, than that apotheosis [glorified example] of anti-intellectualism, the video game?

We can learn a lot from games in ways we cannot from more traditional avenues. Simply by virtue of being entertainment, of course, video games automatically bypass defenses against intellectualism. I posit that there is more to it. Certain games are in a position to take

"I know how to divide. What I want to learn is how to divide and conquer. That could come in handy in one of my video games."

advantage of gamer psychology peculiarities and have players happily engage with potentially educational themes. The game's intention is probably not to teach, and the player's intention is certainty not to learn, but it will happen nonetheless.

Educational video games are represented on a broad continuum. Educational and serious games, those that are exclusive to school computers, are one thing. Mass market puzzles like *Brain Age* and

Typing of the Dead are one more. Another thing entirely is high-profile, sophisticated games like *BioShock, Metal Gear Solid 4,* and *Call of Duty 4: Modern Warfare.*

Clearly, they do not explore their political and philosophical themes—objectivism [a philosophy developed by writer Ayn Rand that encourages self-interest], the war economy, the Middle East conflict—at any level deep enough to substitute the video game for a university education or even the introductory paragraph of a Wikipedia article. They are not academics, nor comprehensive, nor credible.

Graduates will boast that their college professors were Cornel West, John Rawls and Michael Abbott; no one will cite *BiShock,* PhD on his thesis. Compared to video games like *Big Brain Academy* and *Darfur Is Dying,* however, *BioShock* and *Metal Gear Solid* have the potential to be better teachers.

They have a captive audience. At present, the psychological climate of gamers is both frightening and alluring, but it is, amongst other things, the right mindset.

Capitalize on the Hype

Video games are an exceptionally diverse medium, but they suffer from a dearth of creativity within sub-strata. If one likes the fundamental gameplay model of an RPG [role-playing game], they'd better learn to like fantasy and science fiction, because that's all they have. If one likes the visceral action of a shooter, they'd better learn to like World War II and . . . science fiction. If one has only a PlayStation 3 for gaming, they'd better learn to like *Resistance* and *Ratchet & Clank.*

No one bought *Metal Gear Solid 4* solely for Hideo Kojima's unique treatise on private military corporations and the war economy, but a lot of people bought it because it was a major title for the only console they own, and were looking to validate that original purchase. When *Metal Gear Solid* is the only game in town, the player is going to get very well acquainted with it.

More still bought it because they were invested, via message board proxy wars, in the financial success of the PS3 [PlayStation 3] platform. *Metal Gear Solid 4,* as a major exclusive title for a console which attracts relatively few major exclusives, evoked a great protective fervor in its audience [than] it would have done had it appeared simultaneously on Xbox 360, PC, Wii, DS, PS2, PSP, the iPhone and the N-Gage. Or if there were a dozen other titles releasing at the same time—on any platform—with comparable levels of production, positive hype and potential for high sales.

BioShock and *Call of Duty* were not exclusives but, as triple-A titles, they reached such a critical mass of excitement and press that guaranteed their voice would be heard, as hardcore gamers had to play them to stay in the loop.

[Gaming site] 1UP.com's Shawn Elliott wondered recently why Monolith's *Project Origin* generates less hype than Guerilla Games' *Killzone 2*, when Monolith has the better track record with *F.E.A.R.* and *Condemned,* more to show of *Project Origin* itself, and no major PR blunder like *Killzone 2*'s "possibly real" pre-rendered footage at E3 [the Electronic Entertainment Expo, a trade show for the computer and video game industries] 2005.

FAST FACT

At least 10 percent of the nation's twenty-five hundred school districts use mainstream video games for learning, including *Civilization, Railroad Tycoon,* and *Dance Dance Revolution,* according to *Businessweek.*

The disproportionate levels of enthusiasm are because *Project Origin* is coming to the 360, the PS3 and the PC. Neither it nor *F.E.A.R.* before it are able to inspire the zealotry associated with flagship titles for the Sony consoles, which the Killzone series can enjoy. *Killzone 2* has a dedicated audience that *Project Origin* doesn't, and so it has a chance—that it shouldn't waste but probably will—to talk about something important, to teach.

Guerilla, Kojima, 2K and Infinity Ward have gamers right where a teacher would die to have them. Gamers in the console war mentality are fastidious, enamored and strangely protective of their subject matter, and hyper-attentive to every detail in every screenshot, press release, and NPD [new product development] chart. They're primed to absorb information.

These developers, of course, don't have a teacher's benevolence, and if their students are learning anything practical, it's because they're being manipulated. They won't, however, be any less engaged. This is condescending. Yet gamers are far more amenable learning about private military corporations when the source is a crazy anime about clones and nanotech rather than an international relations class they don't want to be in.

A *Time* magazine article on Mark Twain had Yale law professor Stephen E. Carter observing that "Twain melded his attacks on slavery and prejudice into tales that were on the surface about something else entirely. He drew his readers into the argument by drawing them into the story." *BioShock* does the same thing. Twain's intellectual subversion, however, is rendered inert when his books become part of the classroom.

We're not in a classroom. We're in an arena of spectacle, and while we bemoan all the fanboy bullshit, the hype, the perfect scores, the jaw-dropping graphics, all these little things that are so symptomatic of the race to the bottom, they are still what secures our attention, and that's the first step.

Imagine if that compulsiveness and fanaticism ever translated to those high school English students, who'd form an appreciation society around *Huckleberry Finn,* ready to defend it to the death. Developers have never had a better opportunity to found their game on real-world subtext. At the moment we don't see the mainstream video game as preachy, or work, or a lecture, and so we will listen.

This is the same phenomenon which spontaneously ignites in three million gamers an interest in fitness. Is *Wii Fit* attracting fitness buffs, or gamers interested mostly in the Wii, and with gaming trends? Thomas Jefferson would have read all the airport thrillers he could have got his hands on if only they had existed.

Let the Game Sell the Message

Narrative-heavy video games are almost exclusively airport thrillers. Some of those airport thrillers, though, like *Metal Gear Solid,* like *BioShock,* like *Call of Duty,* touch upon serious issues, perhaps introducing the very concepts to a certain fraction of their audience. These games are not didactic [instructive]—they're entertainment, first and foremost—but, at their best, serve as the preamble to an appendix of further recommended reading.

Call of Duty 4, however subliminally, can make gamers more interested than they previously had been in the current Middle East situation, and from *Call of Duty* it's [journalists] George Packer and Thomas Ricks and Seymour Hersh, and from there it's so much closer to actually doing something about it in the real world.

Call of Duty is not a history lesson. It doesn't need to be; in fact it needs to be so little. All it has to be is that fleeting spark that lights the fire. To be sure, it will sound bizarre to remark some day, while shaking hands in the White House, that this was all made possible by *Call of Duty 4*, that renowned catalyst for positive social change.

Games Can Make Learning Fun

Yet why should the indignity in that statement matter to anyone? Surely the ends justify the means. Video games can be gateways to higher learning. Is it idealistic? Sure. But the base repudiation of idealism is so often used as a shield against saying anything interesting. Anti-idealism is what keeps triple-A games generic, and the reversal of that trend should already be a good enough target.

Compare the social value of these games to that of *Halo* or *Oblivion*. They're just as entertaining, but they are not relevant to any humanitarian or political discussion, and are certainly not literary. *The Wire* and *The West Wing* will not reform government but they will challenge and galvanize their viewers.

Now imagine if *The Wire* was one of five titles available for Blu-Ray at launch and how much larger a pulpit it would have. *Blacksite: Area 51* had something provocative to say, but unfortunately for Midway and designer Harvey Smith, it wasn't an exclusive nor did it have the promotion or production of *BioShock*. *Blacksite* was marketed on its message (at least by Smith, and to a greater degree than *Call of Duty* or *Metal Gear Solid*) and that selling point was evidently not as exciting to gamers.

The game, commendably, still said what Smith wanted it to, but it never reached the audience it could have, because subtext doesn't sell. It's the blood and the psychic abilities that draw gamers in. Sometimes teaching is like a magic trick. You need to hide the blackboard.

We still see video games, the commercial blockbusters, as entertainment first and art second. One can read as much into the philosophy of *BioShock* as they like, but it can still be experienced as just a fun shooter. In this narrow historical window, video games can make learning fun. They can be a podium for developers to share with gamers their ideologies; their interests; their bookcases.

[William] Shakespeare and [John] Milton quotes read as superficial gravitas through overuse, but *Deus Ex's* inclusion of passages by the less-ubiquitous [British writer] G.K. Chesterton surely spurred players to investigate Chesterton's body of work. That's the reaction that video games can shoot for but so rarely do.

A Call to Video Game Designers

It's not all about saving the world. We can still discover things like objectivism, Chesterton and BMI [the body mass index] through video games. With the second *Guitar Hero*, Harmonix, then holding a monopoly on the franchise, had the chance to include whatever music they wanted, lesser-known bands that without *Guitar Hero* would never have drawn a massive audience of video game players. The tracklist could have been limited entirely to early-eighties post-punk because maybe that was what the developer happened to like.

Games like those in the Guitar Hero series expose players to lesser-known bands and allow them to choose their own music.

Even if gamers didn't think they would be interested in the music, they would buy it anyway because it was the only new *Guitar Hero* they had. They may have found in *Mission of Burma* or *The Fall* something that they liked, and have *Guitar Hero* to thank. Now, the Guitar Hero and Rock Band franchises are bloated and overexposed, and gamers might as well pick a SKU [stock-keeping unit; i.e., a particular product] based on what bands they recognize, and never discover anything new.

In time, this will happen to video games at every level. There will be twenty games that look like *BioShock* and gamers will choose the one with the best graphics and AI [artificial intelligence] over the one that is sort of a consideration of philosophy and society. Which is why it's important to act now.

This is a call to developers. [Entrepreneur] Ken Levine cared about objectivism and he said so. What moves you outside of games? What matters so much to you, but because you make shooters instead of social policy or literary journals, you never thought [we] the audience [were] receptive? Rock music? Mark Twain? Calculus? We're listening. Talk to us.

EVALUATING THE AUTHOR'S ARGUMENTS:

Duncan Fyfe is an insider in the video game world. In your opinion, how does this shape his argument?

Video Game–Style Software Is Not an Educational Cure-All

Evany Thomas

> *"All the bells and whistles and electronic beeping in the world can't take the place of a skilled, enthusiastic teacher."*

In the following article Evany Thomas argues that educational video games are not as effective as good teachers. She cites a Department of Education study that found little to no difference in students who used educational software and those who did not. And besides being expensive, Thomas argues, educational software creates passive students who expect to be constantly entertained. Thomas is the author of *The Secret Language of Sleep*.

AS YOU READ, CONSIDER THE FOLLOWING QUESTIONS:

1. In the book *The Flickering Mind: The False Promise of Technology in the Classroom and How Learning Can Be Saved*, educators had high hopes for what earlier technologies?
2. What is the cost of a single "Curriculum on Wheels" box, according to the article?
3. The Mr. Bighead song "Money, Souls, and Soil" is geared to teach kids about what, according to Thomas?

Evany Thomas, "The Trouble with Mr. Bighead: Reconsidering the Effectiveness of Educational Software," *Edutopia*, June 27, 2007. Copyright © 2010 The George Lucas Educational Foundation. Reproduced by permission of the author.

The beeping, blinking world of educational software took a blow recently when researchers released their findings from a $10 million study charting the effectiveness of technology in the classroom. It appears computer-based products such as LeapTrack, SmartMath, KnowledgeBox, and other favorites don't actually have the positive impact so many users had hoped for, at least when it comes to test scores.

This isn't the first time technology has failed to measure up to its space-age promise. There's a long tradition of "latest technologies" being trotted out as educational cure-alls. As Todd Oppenheimer notes in his book *The Flickering Mind: The False Promise of Technology in the Classroom and How Learning Can Be Saved,* educators had similarly high hopes for the revolutionizing powers first of radio, then moving pictures, and then television. Those earlier technological advancements also sounded great on paper but bombed when it came to dramatically speeding up the learning process, deepening students' understanding, or improving test scores.

FAST FACT

Teachers are using Nintendo's Wii system for a variety of subjects, including physics, gym, and geography.

Time and again, we learn what we half-suspected all along: All the bells and whistles and electronic beeping in the world can't take the place of a skilled, enthusiastic teacher. And just like the books and chalkboards of yore, these new systems are only as good as the teacher who wields them.

These findings come with economic implications, of course. A recent *New York Times* article lists the cost of a single "Curriculum on Wheels" box (another of the latest techno-teaching solutions) in the $6,800 range. But perhaps more troubling is the side effect of some of this software. It seems that introducing these animated, click-and-learn systems into the classroom rewires kids' brains and rearranges their expectations, creating a passive audience of students who want to be entertained and expect their teachers to be more animated than the Mr. Bighead character leaping on the screen.

As someone who can't enter a television-enhanced bar or restaurant without being driven to distraction—no matter how boring the programming (hello, golf!)—I can fully sympathize with the rewired students. As for Mr. Bighead himself, I understand his charms: I have childhood memories of his old-time analogs, from the puppets (Big Bird) to the cartoon characters (Yuck Mouth) who took up permanent residence in my brain with their catchy, semieducational songs belted out from my television. . . .

"Our gymnasium is being repaired so we played sports games on our computers."

"Our gymnasium is being repaired so we played sports games on our computers," cartoon by Aaron Bacall. www.CartoonStock.com. © Aaron Bacall. Reproduction rights obtainable from www.CartoonStock.com.

Critics of educational software say that many such programs are more entertaining than educational.

Too Much Entertainment, Not Enough Education

But there's a key difference, a topically academic distinction, between the cheese-and-cracker-wagon-wheel-rolling [character] Timer of my childhood and the Mr. Bighead of today. Timer, Big Bird, and Interplanet Janet were government-funded glimmers of education slipped in between the Saturday-morning cartoons I watched at home. But Mr. Bighead is the star of a commercially sold and dubiously educational cartoon slipped between lessons of the school day. One is education masking itself as entertainment, while the other feels dangerously close to entertainment masking itself as education.

And even if Mr. Bighead's catchy sing-along "Money, Souls, and Soil" rap does manage to teach a few kids why Europeans immigrated to America, is it worth having him otherwise rob the teacher of the classroom's focus and attention—which were hard enough to win even before Mr. Bighead came onto the scene?

When I think back on my own school days, some of my crispest, clearest memories are of my teachers. Mrs. Sieg, who always wore her long, white hair in a trademark teacher bun, totally transformed me in fourth grade with the book *The Once and Future King.* Mr. Beans, my third-grade teacher and a complete bicycle-safety nut, taught me the hand signals for "left," "right," and "thinking about stopping." And Mrs. Cooper's infectious obsession with the Mayan Indians, which ate up most of sixth grade, is the reason for my still-burning desire to visit the Yucatan.

Maybe it's true, as one teacher in the *Times* article said about her charges, that "the kids are so into the video games. We have to entertain them, or we lose them." But it's hard to imagine Mr. Bighead developing a fantastic—which is to say human—obsession with the ruins at Chichen Itza and all the kids getting fired up about Mayan architecture as a result.

Maybe technology will one day become so advanced that it will be possible to duplicate the inspirational, transformative powers of a trained, thoughtful, and inspired teacher. Maybe, in the not-so-distant future, software will be intuitive enough to notice when an unexpected topic sparks a kid's interest, and then simultaneously guide that student through a chain of related topics. Maybe they'll find a way to make educational software that's both affordable and demonstrably effective at improving student performance. Until then, I'm entirely satisfied with my Mr. Bighead-less, teacher-taught education.

EVALUATING THE AUTHOR'S ARGUMENTS:

Evany Thomas's argument combines statistics and references to other articles with a more personal approach. Does this mix work well, in your opinion? To which type of argument are you more responsive?

On-Screen Violence Causes Aggressive Behavior

United Press International

"He told the gathering of cops and teachers that the video games are teaching young children to do the same thing he taught would-be soldiers to do."

In the following viewpoint United Press International reports on the views of retired army lieutenant colonel David Grossman. Grossman, who was a former psychology professor at West Point and the founder of the science of "killology"—the study of the psychological cost of learning to kill—informs listeners that killing is a difficult thing to do, and in the military soldiers have to be trained to do it. However, in much the same way in civilian society, violent video games teach children to kill, partly through rewarding rather than punishing them for killing on-screen humans and humanoids.

"Commentary: Violent Video Games No Better Than Porno Films," United Press International, October 23, 2000, p. 1008296u4056. Reproduced by permission.

1. At what age does Grossman believe that a person should be legally allowed to play violent video games?
2. What has the video game industry done to regulate itself, according to the article?
3. What are the faults of the video game rating system, according to Grossman?

In the mind of David Grossman, a video game such as those in the Duke Nukem series with its graphic violence and hints of sex is no better than a pornographic film.

Grossman, a retired army lieutenant colonel-turned-activist against video games who has written the book "Stop Teaching Our Kids to Kill," would like to see laws restricting the ability of young children to get at either.

"If you go to Toys 'R' Us, you can find Duke Nukem action figures and I think that is terrible," Grossman said. "What would people think if they went to a toy store and found *Debbie Does Dallas* (a graphic sex film of the 1970s) action figures for sale?

"They wouldn't stand for those toys. Why should they settle for toys glorifying graphic violence?" he said.

In the Duke Nukem series, the title character is supposed to be a human male killing off a race of aliens who are trying to conquer Earth. The Nukem character goes around with a huge arsenal of weapons, shooting everything in sight. He also likes to stop in strip clubs, where shootouts with aliens can also take place while computer-generated strippers bump and grind away.

Grossman said that game is not unique. Many video games also encourage players to blaze away with their weapons to win, with the occasional innocent victim being sacrificed in the name of victory.

The anticipated U.S. debut this week [October 23, 2000] of Playstation 2 game consoles by Sony is a negative for Grossman, who said, "It will only enhance the graphicness of the killing."

Grossman—who served in the army Rangers and helped train soldiers to make the psychological adjustments necessary for them to kill another human being in combat—spoke to a gathering last week of Chicago police officials, educators and social workers.

He told the gathering of cops and teachers that the video games are teaching young children to do the same thing he taught would-be soldiers to do.

"You need to understand that killing is a difficult thing to train to do," Grossman said. "But these games are doing that by encouraging young people to think it is a good thing to shoot at other human forms."

He said he sees the video games as different from toys such as cap pistols or other war games that children sometimes play.

"It's not just a high-tech cap gun," Grossman said.

"In those forms of play, if someone really gets hurt, someone else gets in trouble. A child learns the view that really hurting someone is wrong. The value of human life forms is reinforced.

"But in these games, if you blow someone's head off, you get extra points," he said. "You don't get in trouble, you get rewarded. It's very dysfunctional play."

Video game industry officials have said they should be allowed to regulate themselves. The Entertainment Software Review Board already has created a rating system for such games, with the most graphic being rated "M" (mature) or "AO" (adults only).

But that rating system, Grossman said, is inadequate because many parents don't know it exists. And the ratings, he thinks, are vague.

"It's deceptive. 'M' is the video game equivalent of (the movie rating) NC-17. That's what we called 'X' rated movies.

"Many people might think that 'M' equals (the movie rating) 'R,' but it does not. 'M' equals 'X,'" Grossman said. "Even if it's not sexual, it's a murder simulator, and that's just as bad."

Grossman added, "Besides, kids reading those ratings won't believe them. Every kid will see the 'M' rating and say 'I'm mature enough.'"

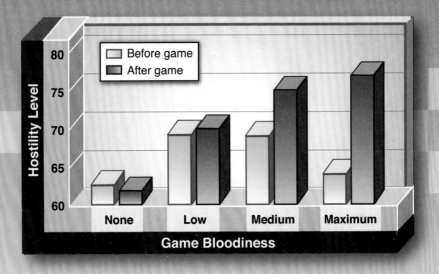

Player Hostility and Game Bloodiness

Taken from: C. Barlett, R. Harris, and C. Bruey, "The Effect of the Amount of Blood in a Violent Video Game on Aggression, Hostility, and Arousal," *Journal of Experimental Social Psychology*, vol. 44, no. 3, 2008.

Grossman supports efforts of political officials who want to restrict access of the more violent video games to people over the age of 18.

"It's really no different than the laws that already exist that ban children from having tobacco, alcohol, guns, sex, cars and pornography," he said.

Various congressmen, including Democratic vice presidential candidate Joseph Lieberman, a Connecticut senator, have held hearings in Washington to determine if federal laws are needed to regulate the content of video games.

Illinois Attorney General Jim Ryan has conducted sting operations of retailers to determine which ones were selling violent games to children under 17 and also has pressured several retail chains—including Kmart, Target and Wal-Mart—to check for identification when selling such games, to ensure they are sold only to adults.

Ryan's request is not mandatory—the Best Buy and Babbage's retail chains have ignored it to date.

Some people concerned about the violent and/or sexual content of many video games think that game content should be regulated by the government.

Grossman supports the efforts but particularly favors an attempt by Indianapolis city officials to require video arcade owners to label games with graphic violence or sexual content.

It also called for fines against arcade owners who allow minors to play those games unless a parent has given written permission to the child.

"That is the ideal solution," Grossman said, adding he was upset that a federal appeals court in Chicago last week struck down parts of the law, saying they were unenforceable.

"It was a good way of dealing with the situation because it would force parents to pay attention to what their children are doing, and to make the decisions about what is appropriate," Grossman said. "It's like if I were to give a sip of beer to my grandbaby. It ought to be my business.

"But if you try to sell beer to my grandbaby, that ought to be my business as well."

EVALUATING THE AUTHORS' ARGUMENTS:

Compare the opinions of David Grossman in this viewpoint by United Press International to those of Christopher J. Ferguson, the author of the following viewpoint. Which person's credentials suggest a more credible argument? Is any bias evident in the argument/opinion of either? Explain your answer.

Violent Video Games Do Not Cause Violence

"There is no good evidence linking violent video games with aggression, violent behavior or any other 'harm.'"

Christopher J. Ferguson

In the following article Christopher J. Ferguson argues that violent video games do not cause people to be violent. According to research, he writes, frequent players of violent video games are no more likely to commit violent crimes than non-gamers. He also notes that in the past decade, violent video games have skyrocketed in popularity while violent crime rates have fallen. Ferguson is a psychologist and an assistant psychology professor at Texas A&M University.

AS YOU READ, CONSIDER THE FOLLOWING QUESTIONS:

1. According to the author, have violent crime rates skyrocketed since the early 1990s?
2. Ferguson lists six different reasons why a child might be violent. Name three of them.
3. An "M" rating on a video game is roughly equivalent to which movie rating, according to the author?

The release of the game *Grand Theft Auto IV (GTA)* has set off the expected cascade of concern from society's moral crusaders. As a psychologist and researcher of violent video games, I am used to the spectacle. Rhode Island [attorney general] Patrick Lynch has added his voice to the cacophony [uproar], warning parents to be wary of *GTA*. Mr. Lynch's comments that parents ought to be informed about the content of video games that they buy for their children is an excellent suggestion, yet I fear that these comments may mistakenly contribute to the uninformed hysteria that surrounds modern video games. I believe that parents who may consider buying a Mature-rated game such as *GTA* for their teens or children should be aware of all the facts.

First, there is no good evidence linking violent video games with aggression, violent behavior or any other "harm." In my own research I consistently find that violent games are not related to violent criminal behaviors or aggression. Frequent players of violent games are no more likely to commit violent crimes than non-gamers.

A recent Secret Service report on school shooters found that few school shooters had unusual interest in violent video games and may have consumed fewer violent games than normal teen males. Indeed, the recent [2007] Virginia Tech shooter did not play violent video games at all, a rarity among young males. Unfortunately the social-science community is largely responsible for the public misconception that violent games and violent behaviors are related. Social scientists have simply failed to communicate to the public the severe limitations and contradictory findings of much of the existing science.

Violent video games have skyrocketed in popularity since the early 1990s. Since that time, in the United States and Canada, violent-crime rates have plummeted. We can be sure that violent video games have not sparked a violence epidemic because there is no violence epidemic. If your child is violent, this is most likely because of genetics,

> **FAST FACT**
>
> *Grand Theft Auto IV* sold more than 6 million copies in its first week of release, making video game history. The game brought in $300 million, which is more than the movie *Iron Man*, which opened the same week did.

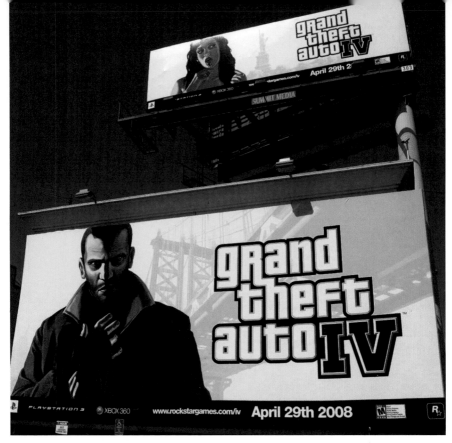

Mass marketing of violent video games has caused them to skyrocket in popularity. However, the author points out that, contrary to general expectations, the rate of violent crime has fallen in both Canada and the United States.

the child's personality, family violence and neglect, or poverty and the economy, in roughly that order.

Second, contrary to the claims of many anti-game advocates, *GTA* does not "award points" for antisocial acts. Few video games today "award points" for much of anything, instead offering players a wide range of options, sometimes including antisocial acts. Storytelling is the focus, not points. In *GTA* antisocial acts are punished via fines, arrest or shooting by in-game police officers. *GTA* doesn't stop players from engaging in antisocial acts, yet it doesn't require them either. If your child is shooting police officers in the game, that's because your child chose to do so, not because the game required it.

Parents Need to Be Involved

Third, *GTA* is not designed for kids. It's an adult-oriented game. Whether you should let your child or teen play such a game is entirely your decision. Consider *GTA* equivalent to a violent R-rated movie. If your child already has significant problems with violence, you might rethink buying the game. For most kids, the decision is entirely a moral one, not a scientific one. Parents should be comfortable making their own moral decisions. You are already fully empowered to do so and don't require legislative permission. Read the game ratings, they're right on the front of the box. An "M" rating is roughly equivalent to an R-rated movie.

Fourth, some research indicates that playing violent video games specifically may improve visual-spatial cognition. These cognitive tasks are used in careers such as engineering, architecture and surgery. For reasons that are poorly understood, violent games appear to increase these abilities, whereas non-violent games do not. Naturally, the violence need not be as brutal as in *GTA*, and it is probably the fast action and decision-making required in violent games rather than the violence itself that boosts these skills. Nonetheless, this is one facet often left out of the video-game debate.

Fifth, if you decide to buy *GTA* or other violent games for your kids, play it with them. That's right, get right in there and learn the game yourself. If you do allow violent video games, this will give you an opportunity to talk with your kids about violence and crime. You can discuss that the behaviors in the game are unacceptable in real life, a message made more credible by your familiarity with youth culture. The best influence you can have on your kids is through time spent with them.

Video games, even violent ones, are as good an opportunity as any.

EVALUATING THE AUTHOR'S ARGUMENTS:

Christopher J. Ferguson uses a methodical argument, listing his points, one to five. Name one advantage and one disadvantage to this sort of argument, and explain your answer.

Chapter 2

How Do Video Games Affect Players' Health?

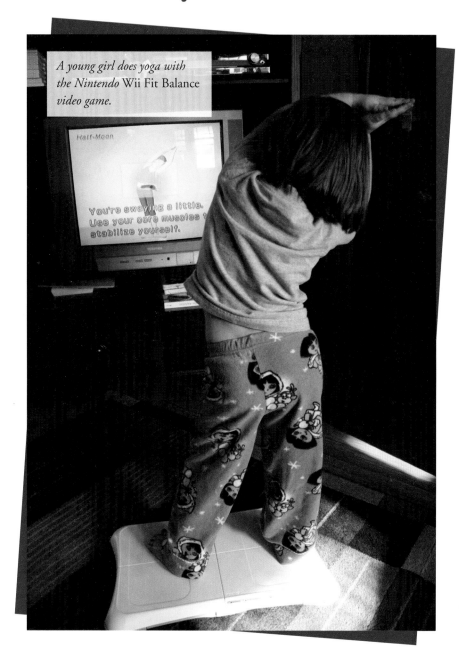

A young girl does yoga with the Nintendo Wii Fit Balance video game.

Viewpoint
1

Video Game Playing Can Improve Health

Jodai Saremi

"Anything that motivates children and adults alike to work up a sweat and encourages long-term play, week after week, should be at the top of any trainer's list of weight loss secrets."

In the following viewpoint Jodai Saremi argues that active video games such as *Wii Fit, Eye Toy*, and *Dance Dance Revolution* can be valuable tools in improving health. Games are a good addition to a fitness plan because they encourage movement, make exercise fun, and allow players to chart their progress, she asserts. Additionally, writes Saremi, video games have great potential to aid in patient rehabilitation. Saremi is certified in group exercise and personal training and is a contributing editor to *American Fitness* magazine.

Jodai Saremi, "Win or Lose: It's How You Play the Game," *American Fitness,* vol. 27, September/October 2009, pp. 12–14. Copyright © 2009 American Fitness Magazine. Reproduced by permission.

AS YOU READ, CONSIDER THE FOLLOWING QUESTIONS:
1. Public schools in ten states have incorporated what game into their physical education curricula?
2. What is the average heart rate while playing *Dance Dance Revolution*, according to research cited by the author?
3. What is another word for visually induced motion sickness, according to Saremi?

You know you're in trouble when your TV tells you you're obese. San Diego Padres baseball player, Heath Bell, is one of a growing number of people who got a wakeup call from a fitness video game. His children's *Wit Fit* made his onscreen character obese. Heeding the 2005 Pediatric Obesity Conference's dire warning that "This is the first generation of kids who are more likely to die before their parents due to obesity and its related diseases," the companies that contributed to the sedentary lifestyle of the young have developed games to get kids up off the couch and moving. "Exergaming," targets adults and children alike with video games that encourage physical fitness.

Obviously, if kids are moving while engaged in a videogame, they aren't just staring at a screen and snacking, so they must be getting some healthful benefits, right? In fact, studies showed that kids complied better with an exercise prescription if it involved computer or video gaming because their interest was captured for longer periods of time—they were being entertained as they worked to lose weight.

Dependent on virtual reality technology, these games use software-generated simulation of a real environment for training, education and gaming. The games are interactive and customized to each user. In researching what was available specifically for exercise gaming, three game systems came up repeatedly: Wii Fit by Nintendo, the PlayStation II Eye Toy: Kinetic by Sony and Dance Dance Revolution (DDR) by Konami Digital Entertainment (released in 1991 in Japan).

Video Games as Part of an Exercise Plan

Eye Toy uses video capture technology: A camera embeds the user's image within a simulated environment so that it is possible to interact with animated graphics while standing in front of a monitor or screen. Anything you do, such as kick, punch, jump, your character onscreen will also do. The *Wii Fit* uses a Balance Board as the main interface between user and game. Its sensors can read your weight and also how you shift your weight. A handheld remote control allows you to enter additional data to personalize your avatar onscreen. The remote is also necessary to detect other movements. *DDR* employs a sensor mat to track foot position as the user faces a screen and follows brightly lit cues set to music.

Many gyms use virtual training on stationary bikes where the exercisers watch a video screen as they ride through virtual terrain and interact with the onscreen images to reach their goals and increase scores. And in April 2009, Gold's Gym released the more intense

As part of an exercise regimen, a father and his children work out using the Dance Dance Revolution *video game.*

Cardio Workout from Ubisoft for Wii consoles to encourage those who have progressed beyond the Wii Fit games to "mix it up" with their gym-based workout routine.

Dr. Ernie Medina (preventive care specialist at Beaver Medical Group in Redlands, Calif.) touts PS2 *Eye Toy, DDR,* and *Wii Fit* as great ways to motivate people. He has opened the XRtainment Zone using *DDR* and other fitness games to attract those who would otherwise never set foot in a gym. According to Serious Games Source Web site, some critics denounce these games as subpar though, because they feel that users are not really playing with strategy, which is what diehard videogamers look for.

> ## FAST FACT
>
> A child's heart rate can reach 130 beats a minute while playing Wii, as opposed to 83 beats a minute for a child playing sedentary games, according to a study by Liverpool John Moores University.

The medical community has seen the potential for exergaming not only for weight loss, but also as an adjunct to traditional rehabilitation modalities. Experiments on a wide age range of patients have shown that the exergaming format is enjoyed by all; exercise bikes and *Eye Toy*–type technology can assist in rehabilitating patients with everything from cerebral palsy to strokes or those with other types of neural damage. Patients work on balance, mobility, posture, eye-hand coordination, stamina, strength and improving their sense of independence.

Another advantage to using virtual augmented exercise gaming is that progress can be measured accurately. Doctors and therapists can individualize treatments and objectively measure behavior in challenging yet safe environments where they are in strict control over stimulus delivery.

The Benefits of Games

As trainers and athletes, you might wonder how these techno-workouts measure up to "real" (traditional) physical activity. Before recommending them to your clients, find out if they produce results; how easy the games are to use; and if they are sustainable and safe.

Before skepticism gets in the way of your objectivity, note that public schools in 10 states have incorporated *DDR* into their physical education curricula. Dr. George Graham, professor of kinesiology at Penn State University, and Stephen Yang, faculty at [State University of New York] Cortland, found that the average heart rate while playing *DDR* for 45 minutes was 144, compared to a resting heart rate of 60 to 70 beats per minute. This type of research finding alone confirms active video gaming has more health benefits than sedentary games.

The *Eye Toy* definitely has an edge on the cool-factor with the ability to control the game by tapping on the virtual screen. Whatever appears on the screen, you can "touch" with your computer-generated mirror image and the object will react.

Wii Fit, on the other hand, employs a Balance Board on which the user stands to play games or exercise. Data picked up from the user's foot pressure are transmitted to the Wii programs. As a nod to fitness and health alike, both the *Eye Toy: Kinetic* and the *Wii Fit* allow users to enter data such as age, gender, height and weight, which is then used to calculate body mass index (BMI) and calories burned. Both *Wii* and *Eye Toy* set up special 12-week programs where users choose a virtual "trainer" to direct the exercises and encourage progress. That's where the similarities end. Although both have cardio, toning and mind-body workouts, the biggest difference between *Wii Fit* and *Eye Toy: Kinetic* lies in the graphics and the style in which the workouts are conducted.

Fun for Adults and Kids

Wii Fit is geared directly toward children. Cartoon caricatures' movements are accompanied by a carnival-type, action music soundtrack. Users (known as Wii Miis) appear onscreen as mini doll-like mannequins. A remote controller must be held to make activity choices onscreen or whenever an exercise doesn't require the Board. Certain types of exercises, such as running and Stepping, and all the balance games, employ the use of the Wii Mii avatars. But, during the strength training and yoga sessions, a human trainer avatar demonstrates the moves, and then does the exercise with you.

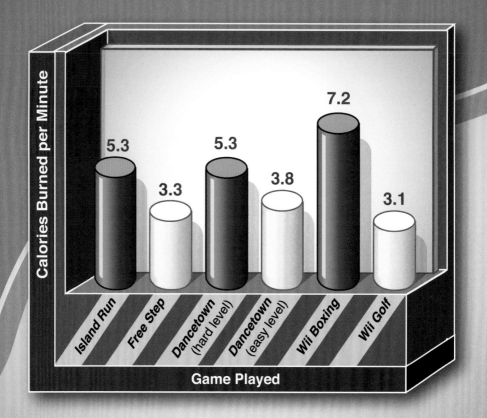

Calories Burned While Gaming

Calories Burned per Minute

5.3 — Island Run
3.3 — Free Step
5.3 — Dancetown (hard level)
3.8 — Dancetown (easy level)
7.2 — Wii Boxing
3.1 — Wii Golf

Game Played

Taken from: University of Wisconsin, La Crosse Exercise and Health Program, 2009, University of Wisconsin, 2008, and the American Council on Exercise.

Any exercise requiring balance is well-adapted for the Wii Balance Board. Encouragement is given if you perform well and directions for improvement are given if you perform poorly. A "Fit Bank" tracks time spent on the Wii so that new exercises can be earned.

Eye Toy: Kinetic's avatars are human and their personalities have been developed to appeal to adults. This live-action game translates movements into controlling elements of the game. When you kick or punch at a target, you earn points. When you duck out of the way of a flying object, you earn points. You are one of the avatars in the game. Part of the appeal of exergaming, is that it engages the participants' minds more than walking on a treadmill or swimming laps in a pool.

In the *Eye Toy: Kinetic's* personal trainer mode, programs come complete with warm-ups and stretches and grades at the end of every routine, plus at the end of every week. Proper alignment and good form are enhanced with the use of guiding lights and motion arcs to follow.

Room for Improvement

The biggest drawbacks to the *Eye Toy* are that it requires a large space to move around and a simple background so that the camera doesn't read the couch, for example, as a participant in the game. Lighting is also important. *Wii Fit's* limiting factor is the Balance Board. Although the Board is very useful for Stepping routines, exercise intensity is restricted by the fixed height of the Board and the inability to jump on it. For some users with large feet or significant girth, the Board may pose a tripping hazard, since the Board is relatively short and narrow.

Studies on the side effects of using VR [virtual reality] have shown differing results depending on the type of technology. [Researcher Sarah] Nichols reported some complaints of discomfort from head-mounted displays, difficulty adjusting to the 3-D hand-held devices, a fear of getting entangled in connector cables and dissatisfaction with visual displays. Japanese researchers related users feeling motion sick during immersion in a virtual environment on a bike due to the combined effects of visual stimuli and performance of physical activity on the vestibular and ocular autonomic nervous systems. In other words, some people were more sensitive to the perceived motion and simultaneous eye movements during virtual exercise sessions. This problem was addressed by having users practice at controlled levels of training and then rest for a prescribed amount of time.

Clinicians, physical therapists and trainers must be aware that vestibular system sensitivity varies from person to person and that some may experience dizziness and nausea that last up to an hour post immersion VR exposure.

However, studies using video capture VR showed no significant concerns for visually induced motion sickness, also known as "cybersickness." None of the healthy participants experienced a level of discomfort that caused them to quit the games.

The bottom line is that *DDR, Eye Toy: Kinetic* and *Wii Fit* are actually home fitness products designed to get people moving. They can be applied to improve health and healthcare. Anything that motivates children and adults alike to work up a sweat and encourages long-term play, week after week, should be at the top of any trainer's list of weight loss secrets.

EVALUATING THE AUTHOR'S ARGUMENTS:

In your opinion, what is the greatest strength in Jodai Saremi's argument? What is the greatest weakness?

Video Game Playing Has Health Risks

Elsevier Health Sciences

"[Researchers] found measurable correlations between video-game playing and health risks."

There is a link between video game playing and health risks, according to Elsevier Health Sciences in *ScienceDaily* in the following selection. The author cites a study that found that video game players have more health risk factors, including a higher body mass index (BMI) and a greater number of poor mental health days. These findings—combined with earlier studies showing greater levels of introversion, mental health problems, and weight issues—point to a need for further research in how to use video games to promote health, researchers say.

AS YOU READ, CONSIDER THE FOLLOWING QUESTIONS:
1. Why was the Seattle-Tacoma area selected for the study of video game playing, according to the author?
2. Did male or female video game players report greater depression levels, according to the article?
3. List two health risk factors that differentiated video game players from nonplayers, according to the article.

Elsevier Health Sciences, "Links Between Video-Game Playing and Health Risks in Adults Found," *ScienceDaily,* August 18, 2009. www.sciencedaily.com/releases/2009/08/090818083224.htm. The source requests the following acknowledgment: James B. Weaver, III, Darren Mays, Stephanie S. Weaver, Wendi Kannenberg, Gary L. Hopkins, Dogan Eroglu, and Jay M. Bernhardt, "Health-Risk Correlates of Video-Game Playing Among Adults," *American Journal of Preventive Medicine,* vol. 37, October 2009. Reproduced by permission. www.elsevier.com.

W hile video gaming is generally perceived as a pastime for children and young adults, research shows that the average age of players in the United States is 35. Investigators from the Centers for Disease Control and Prevention (CDC), Emory University and Andrews University analyzed survey data from over 500 adults ranging in age from 19 to 90 in the Seattle-Tacoma area on health risks; media use behaviors and perceptions, including those related to video-game playing; and demographic factors. In an article published in the October 2009 issue of the *American Journal of Preventive Medicine*, they found measurable correlations between video-game playing and health risks.

Participants reported whether they were players or nonplayers, and weekly usage was collected. Internet usage was assessed, as was the relative importance of the Internet as a social support. The personal determinants examined in this study included self-assessments of depression, personality, health status, physical and mental health, body mass index (BMI), and poor quality of life. Immersion in media environments was evaluated using the participants' estimates of the time they spent during a typical week surfing the Internet and watching TV, including videos and DVDs. The Seattle-Tacoma area was selected because of its size (13th largest US media market) and its Internet usage level is the highest in the nation.

> # FAST FACT
>
> The average gamer is thirty-five years old, overweight, and depressed, according to a 2009 study from the Centers for Disease Control and Prevention, Emory University, and Andrews University.

A total of 45.1% of respondents reported playing video games. Female video-game players reported greater depression and lower health status than female nonplayers. Male video-game players reported higher BMI and more Internet use time than male nonplayers. The only determinant common to both female and male video-game players was greater reliance on the Internet for social support.

INACTIVITY CENTRE

"Inactivity Centre," cartoon by Nathan Ariss. www.CartoonStock.com. © Nathan Ariss. Reproduction rights obtainable from www.CartoonStock.com.

Substituting "Playlike Activities" for Real Play

Writing in the article, Dr. James B Weaver III, PhD, MPH, National Center for Health Marketing, CDC [Centers for Disease Control and Prevention], Atlanta, states, "As hypothesized, health-risk factors—specifically, a higher BMI and a greater number of poor mental-health days—differentiated adult video-game players from nonplayers. Video-game players also reported lower extraversion, consistent with research on adolescents that linked video-game playing to a sedentary lifestyle and overweight status, and to mental-health concerns. Internet community support and time spent online distinguished adult video-game players from nonplayers, a finding consistent with prior research pointing to the willingness of adult video-game enthusiasts to sacrifice real-world social activities to play video games. The data illustrate the need for further research among adults to clarify how to use digital opportunities more effectively to promote health and prevent disease."

In a commentary in the same issue, Brian A. Primack, MD, EdM, MS, from the University of Pittsburgh School of Medicine, applauds Weaver et al. for focusing on the current popularity of video games

Research has linked excessive video game playing to sedentary and overweight lifestyles in adolescents and adults.

not only among youth, but also among adults. He suggests that many video games are different enough from original forms of play that they may be better defined as "playlike activities." He writes, "There are noteworthy differences between the oldest forms of play (e.g., chase games) and today's 'playlike activities.' These playlike activities may stimulate the right centers of the brain to be engaging. . . . However, the differences between today's 'playlike activities' and original forms of play may illuminate some of the observed health-related correlates discovered by Weaver, et al."

Dr. Primack observes that our greatest challenge will be maintaining the balance: "How do we simultaneously help the public steer away from imitation playlike activities, harness the potentially positive aspects of video games, and keep in perspective the overall place of video games in our society? There are massive, powerful industries promoting many playlike activities. And industry giants that can afford to will successfully tout the potential benefits of health-related products they develop. But who will be left to remind us that—for children and adults alike—Hide-And-Seek and Freeze Tag are still probably what we need most?"

> **EVALUATING THE AUTHORS' ARGUMENTS:**
>
> How do you think Jodai Saremi, the author of the previous viewpoint, would respond to this viewpoint's assertion that playing video games leads to an unhealthy body mass index?

Video Game Addiction Is a Legitimate Addiction

Meghan Vivo

"Video games feed the brain's reward centers in a similar way that drugs or alcohol produce an appealing 'high.'"

In the following article Meghan Vivo argues that video game addiction is a legitimate addiction. She cites a study by Iowa State University and the National Institute on Media and the Family that found that many gamers display the same types of symptoms as addicted gamblers. Addicted gamers play games twice as much as casual gamers, get into more fights, and do poorly in school, she writes. Parents who suspect their child is addicted, writes Vivo, need to limit screen time and, if necessary, seek professional help. Vivo is a writer who specializes in addiction issues. Vivo is employed by the Aspen Education Group, a provider of therapeutic schools and programs.

AS YOU READ, CONSIDER THE FOLLOWING QUESTIONS:

1. According to the Iowa State study cited in the article, roughly how many video game players show signs of addictive behavior?
2. List three of the problems that addicted gamers might suffer from, according to Vivo.
3. What two techniques have been proven effective in helping teens with video game addiction, according to the author?

To all of those who argue video game addiction is a made-up condition, new research presents evidence that may make you reconsider.

Rekindling the debate as to the existence of video game addiction is a recent study from researchers at Iowa State University [ISU] and the National Institute on Media and the Family. The study, which is based on data from a nationwide survey of 1,178 American children and teenagers, aged 8 to 18, found that roughly one in 10 video game players (8.5 percent of American youth) show signs of addictive behavior. Some displayed at least six of 11 symptoms of pathological gambling as defined by the American Psychiatric Association. (Researchers adopted the gambling addiction criteria because there is no current medical diagnosis of video game addiction).

"While the medical community currently does not recognize video game addiction as a mental disorder, hopefully this study will be one of many that allow us to have an educated conversation on the positive and negative effects of video games," said Dr. Douglas Gentile, a developmental psychologist and assistant professor of psychology at ISU.

The Signs of Video Game Addiction

The problem of video game addiction isn't as simple as playing too much or really enjoying video games. Addicted gamers played video games twice as much as casual gamers (24 hours a week), are more than twice as likely to have ADD/ADHD [attention deficit disorder/attention-deficit hyperactivity disorder], get into more physical fights, and have health problems caused by long hours of game play (e.g, hand and wrist pain, poor hygiene, irregular eating habits). Many need treatment to improve their academic performance and return to normal functioning.

> **FAST FACT**
>
> According to the Center for Online Addiction, warning signs for video game addiction include the following: playing for increasing amounts of time, thinking about gaming during other activities, lying to friends and family to conceal gaming, feeling irritable when trying to cut down on gaming, and gaming to escape from real-life problems, anxiety, or depression.

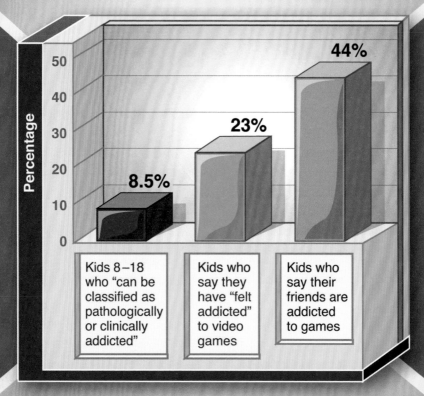

Kids and Video Game Addiction

Percentage

8.5%
Kids 8–18 who "can be classified as pathologically or clinically addicted"

23%
Kids who say they have "felt addicted" to video games

44%
Kids who say their friends are addicted to games

Taken from: Harris Interactive, "Video Game Addiction: Is It Real?" April 2, 2007.

"It's not that the games are bad," said Gentile. "It's not that the games are addictive. It's that some kids use them in a way that is out of balance and harms various other areas of their lives."

It is estimated that 88 percent of young people in the U.S. play video games, indicating that up to three million could be showing signs of addiction. The gamers in the study showed addiction-like symptoms ranging from lying to family and friends about how much they play games and using the games to escape their problems to becoming restless or irritable when they stop playing. For some, video game play affected their academic performance and commitment to spending time with family and friends.

Other symptoms of video game addiction include spending more time and money on video games to feel the same "high," skipping out on responsibilities like household chores or homework to play games, excessive thinking about game play, trying to play less and failing, and stealing games or money to play.

"While video games can be fun and entertaining, some kids are getting into trouble. I continue to hear from families who are concerned about their child's gaming habits. Not only do we need to focus on identifying the problem, but we need to find ways to help families prevent and treat it," said Dr. David Walsh, the president of the National Institute on Media and the Family.

Finding Help for Video Game Addiction

Dubbed by some experts as a "wake-up call" for parents, this research will likely spark greater awareness of the problem of video game addiction. But what is a concerned parent to do? Ban video games from the home? Seek professional help?

Video game addicts participate in a therapy session at a clinic for game addicts in the Netherlands.

The American Academy of Pediatrics currently recommends that children should limit "screen time" (time spent playing video games, using the computer, or watching television and movies) to one or two hours a day of "quality programming." If your child is playing significantly more than this, or if video or computer games are negatively affecting his school or personal life, professional help may be in order.

Although the U.S. is lagging behind countries like South Korea, which boasts more than 100 clinics to treat video game addiction, there are a growing number of treatment options available to American youth. Video games feed the brain's reward centers in a similar way that drugs or alcohol produce an appealing "high." As such, treatment for video game addiction often centers on the same principles as treatment for drug or alcohol addiction.

Video game addiction is often a symptom of an underlying emotional or psychological issue such as depression or anxiety, and sometimes goes hand in hand with defiance, ADHD, and other conditions. In these cases, the child needs a treatment program that will address both video game addiction and any co-occurring emotional or behavioral issues.

Wilderness therapy programs and therapeutic boarding schools have proven effective in helping teens with video game addiction find joy and excitement in healthier ways. With guidance from therapists and teachers, teens work to achieve balance in their lives, finding academic success, emotional fulfillment, and plenty of opportunities for friends and healthy fun.

EVALUATING THE AUTHOR'S ARGUMENTS:

Meghan Vivo works for a company that provides professional therapy for addictions, including video game addiction. Does this influence the credibility of her argument? Why or why not?

Video Game Addiction Is Not a True Addiction

"The notion of video game addiction has no official support from the medical or mental health establishment."

Brandon Erickson

In the following essay Brandon Erickson argues that video game addiction is not a true addiction because it does not meet the American Psychiatric Association's criteria for addiction. Video game players do not have the withdrawal symptoms and tolerance characteristic of substance abuse, writes Erickson. Likewise, comparisons to gambling addiction are flawed, he argues, because video game players do not fall into destructive cycles of betting more to win back losses. Erickson, a *Star Wars* video game champion, holds a master's degree in counseling psychology.

AS YOU READ, CONSIDER THE FOLLOWING QUESTIONS:
1. Name two ways a physiological dependence is characterized, according to the article.
2. According to Erickson, is there scientific proof that gamers experience the same sorts of highs associated with chemical dependence?
3. According to the author, is excessive video game playing usually a symptom of an underlying issue?

The April [2008] issue of the *International Journal of Mental Health and Addiction* contains a fascinating series of articles on the topic of videogame addiction, and in particular, on the question of whether such a thing as videogame addiction even exists. The centerpiece is an article by Richard T.A. Wood entitled "Problems with the Concept of Video Game 'Addiction': Some Case Study Examples." Wood's article is accompanied by three separate critical commentaries, all of which are then followed by another article from Wood responding to some of the issues raised by the commentators. These exchanges make for an interesting discourse on a highly controversial subject.

As Wood points out, the notion of videogame addiction has no official support from the medical or mental health establishment. The American Psychiatric Association's *Diagnostic and Statistical Manual of Mental Disorders* lists criteria for two separate forms of what would commonly be termed "addiction": *substance dependence* and *pathological gambling*. The former usually involves *physiological* dependence, which is characterized by both *tolerance* and *withdrawal* symptoms. The latter, however, is defined primarily in behavioral terms, and as such is frequently used as a template for describing "videogame addiction." The authors agree that this is a flawed approach.

For one thing, problem gambling involves a particular cycle of behavior in which the gambler tries to win back his or her losses by making more bets (i.e., chasing losses). Almost inevitably, this leads to further losses and a continuation of the negative cycle. In addition, research has shown that many pathological gamblers experience a high similar to that which cocaine addicts experience. Of course, videogame playing has nothing to do with betting real money on games of chance. Moreover, there is no scientific proof that gamers experience the same sorts of highs associated with chemical dependence. Clearly, using the criteria for pathological gambling as a model for "videogame addiction" is inappropriate.

A major point of discussion among the authors is the question of whether videogames are inherently addictive. As Wood argues through several case studies, there is little evidence that videogames are inherently addictive or problematic per se; rather, unhealthily excessive videogame playing is often just a symptom of an underlying issue. Wood gives the example of a 10-year-old boy who spends most of his spare time playing *World of Warcraft*. His parents think the game is to blame for his decreased desire to go to school. As it turns out, however, he had recently been the victim of intense bullying and was actually using the game as a safe means of socializing. The game was the symptom, not the cause, of the problem.

How Should Addiction Be Defined?

Although the commentators mostly agree with Wood, they do criticize him on a couple key points. First, since pretty much everyone who suffers from substance dependence also has some underlying

Some experts contend that media hype over video game addiction has caused serious misperceptions of the issue.

mental health disorder, Wood's reasoning could be used to argue that most drug addicts aren't actually addicted, which of course we know to be false. Second, Wood doesn't really supply any proof that videogame addiction doesn't exist; rather, he merely establishes that there isn't any solid proof of it yet. That being said, the authors generally agree that the media hype around videogame "addiction" has caused serious misperceptions around the meaning of the term addiction and led people to draw premature conclusions about the nature of videogames.

In my opinion, this discussion really gets back to how we choose to define "addiction." If we're working from the currently accepted clinical criteria for substance dependence and pathological gambling (the two main reference points), then the notion of videogame "addiction" becomes highly dubious. In fact, the idea of defining specific activities as inherently addictive (e.g., sex, gambling, videogame playing) is a big area of controversy right now in the mental health field. Just because an activity has the potential to be harmful does not necessarily mean it's addictive. That videogames are harmful is far from proven; that they are clinically addictive even less so.

EVALUATING THE AUTHORS' ARGUMENTS:

Compare this essay by Brandon Erickson to the previous one, in which author Meghan Vivo argues that video game addiction is a real addiction. Which essay do you think makes the better argument? Why?

Viewpoint
5

Video Game Playing Can Help Attention Disorders

Rick Hodges

"I have seen distracted kids increase their ability to focus."

In the following article for *ADDitude* magazine, Rick Hodges makes the case for video games as a valuable tool for working with children with attention deficit disorder (ADD) and attention-deficit/hyperactivity disorder (ADHD). Games that are specially designed for children with ADD and ADHD can help children learn to focus and practice self-control, he writes. And, he argues, the games have an advantage over traditional treatments because children enjoy them more. Hodges is a writer specializing in ADD/ADHD issues.

AS YOU READ, CONSIDER THE FOLLOWING QUESTIONS:

1. How is the National Aeronautics and Space Administration technology connected to the types of games described in the article?
2. How long have therapists been using the *Captain's Log* game, according to Hodges?
3. According to the article, "shoot-'em-up" games do not work well for the S.M.A.R.T. BrainGames system. What sorts of games are described as working better?

Most parents fret when their child stays glued to a video game or computer for hours, and they fret for good reason. The gaming industry has been built on violence and frenzied action. In one of the most popular games, *Grand Theft Auto*, players tear drivers out of their cars to mug them, and run over pedestrians.

What if electronic games could help children with attention deficit disorder increase focus for tasks that they find boring?

They might. Parents, therapists, and educators can choose from several new games and devices on the market that may train distracted children or adults to pay more attention. Some connect the user's brain to the home computer through high-tech sensors and allow the person to control the action on the screen, not with a fast finger or a keyboard but with his brain waves. Call it joystick neurofeedback.

Using this method to improve concentration isn't a new idea. Therapists have used the technology for decades. Some games trace their development to National Aeronautics and Space Administration (NASA) technology that measures the brain waves of pilots as they use flight simulators. Today, experts in psychology and technology are finding new ways to link the brain with a computer, and manufacturers are creating software and equipment designed for home users.

Manufacturers and experts agree that the games are only a tool to train a child to pay attention in distracted children, not a treatment for AD/HD. Medication and behavior therapy is the gold standard for improving symptoms of the condition.

"The games have the potential to increase attention stamina," says Rohn Kessler, Ph.D., of Boca Raton, Florida, who works with children with attention deficit. "They aren't a quick fix or a one-step solution, but I have seen distracted kids increase their ability to focus."

ADDitude screened a few of the more intriguing games. Here's what we found.

Captain's Log Ahoy!

With *Captain's Log*, you can become the captain of your own brain, instead of letting impulses and distractions take you off course.

Therapists and educators have used *Captain's Log* to help children and adults with AD/HD and other cognitive challenges since 1985. The software is now used in all 50 states and 23

Children's Satisfaction with Video Game Treatments Versus Computer Program Treatments for ADHD

In one study of treatment for ADHD, children with the disorder controlled either an EEG-equipped simple computer program or an EEG-equipped video game. The EEG (an electroencephalogram, or graphical record of electrical activity in the brain) allowed the children to control the program or game using brain waves. Both groups had similar positive results, and both methods improved the functioning of children with ADHD much more effectively than treatment using medication. However, in a post-treatment survey, children using the video game were more satisfied with their treatment.

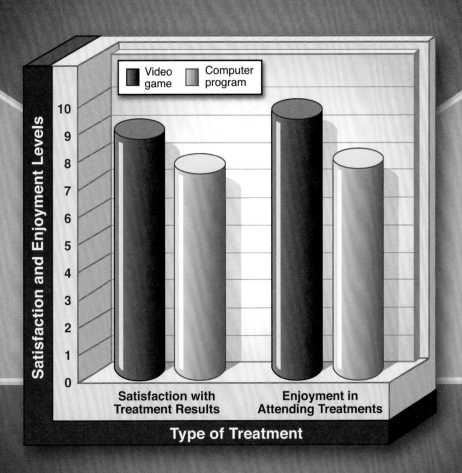

Taken from: NASA and Eastern Virginia Medical School, "Effectiveness of Video Game EEG Neurofeedback on ADHD," 2000. www.smartbraintech.com.

foreign countries, according to the manufacturer, BrainTrain of Richmond, Virginia.

BrainTrain calls *Captain's Log* a "computerized mental gym," which works with any standard computer-control device, like a mouse or a keyboard, or with a joystick or game controller. With more than 30 "brain-training" games and exercises, *Captain's Log* offers a variety of options for helping some students improve concentration, memory, and self-control.

How it works. A child or adult chooses which games he wants to play based on his needs, whether it be improving his inattention or controlling impulsive tendencies. Once the user punches in his preference, a game pops up on the screen. You might be required to match two cards from memory or two similarly colored animals. The pace and length of the games are varied, and visual and audio distractions are thrown in to increase the challenge. The program advances to the next level automatically when the student has mastered the previous level. *Captain's Log* generates detailed reports so that professionals or parents can trace a student's progress, and it produces certificates as rewards for students as they improve.

> ## FAST FACT
>
> Games that can be used as part of a "brain-training" program for children with attention deficit disorder and attention-deficit/hyperactivity disorder include the Tony Hawk games *Amped: FreeStyle Snowboarding* and *NASCAR 2009*.

Captain's Log developer Joseph Sandford, a psychologist with a computer programming background, originally created the software to help patients who had traumatic brain injury. Therapists soon realized that it may increase attention in people with AD/HD.

For more information, log on to braintrain.com. A trial version of the software is available.

Play Attention

Peter Freer was frustrated in trying to help his students overcome attention problems. Combining his teaching experience with his background in educational technology, Freer created *Play Attention,* a system that enables children and adults with AD/HD to connect their brain waves directly to a home computer to hone their ability to stay focused.

"They can actually see what's happening to their brain waves as it occurs," says Freer, CEO of Unique Logic + Technology, the Asheville, North Carolina, manufacturer of the game.

How it works. The user puts on a helmet embedded with sensors and learns to control the action on the screen with his brain waves. Focusing on a flying bird causes it to fly higher; distraction causes the bird to fly lower. Another exercise enables a person to work on his long-range focus by building a tower with moving blocks. A challenging exercise involves sitting at the controls of a spaceship, deflecting the white asteroids that are flying toward it. This helps develop discriminatory processing and impulse control.

While a teacher, therapist, or coach can only describe what focus feels like to someone with AD/HD, *Play Attention* lets the user experience what being attentive actually feels like.

A student can even play the game while doing homework. Wearing the helmet and choosing, say, the plane game, the student can do an assignment and gauge his attention level by looking at the plane's flight pattern.

For more information, log on to playattention.com. A demonstration disk is available.

SmartDriver

Sitting behind the wheel of a car can be a dangerous place for someone with impulsive or inattentive behavior, especially a teenage driver without much experience. *SmartDriver* helps any driver, or future driver, with focus problems to keep his thoughts on the road.

The game works with or without a steering wheel for computer driving simulators. "The kids love *SmartDriver* because they get to drive," says Joseph Sandford, who created the game. Unlike the typical driving video game, *SmartDriver* requires patience and responsibility, not a love of hairpin turns. "There are stretches where you have to stay under the speed limit."

How it works. The game isn't a driving simulator—you "drive" the car from outside of the car as in a typical video game, not from inside it—but you must follow the rules of the road and heed speed limits, traffic lights, and other vehicles. Like *Captain's Log*, *SmartDriver* adds enough lights and sounds to keep a young user interested.

For more information, log on to braintrain.com. A trial version of the software is available.

S.M.A.R.T. BrainGames

Instead of designing games for building concentration skills, the S.M.A.R.T. BrainGames system converts any home video or computer game into a neurofeedback device.

Using new technology developed by NASA, the S.M.A.R.T. ("Self Mastery and Regulation Training") BrainGames system includes a state-of-the-art, wireless, handheld game controller. It looks and works like any other game controller, with one exception—it receives brain wave signals from a headset worn by the player.

How it works. The headset tracks the frequency of the user's brain waves while he plays. When the player exhibits low-frequency patters during, say, a car race at the track, his car slows and other cars pass him. That gets his attention, so he concentrates, producing higher-frequency brain waves. His car then speeds up—positive reinforcement for his cerebral change. The idea is that the higher-frequency pattern will continue even after kids stop playing the game.

NASA's tests of the technology showed that it works about as well as traditional biofeedback equipment used in clinics, but with an important twist—children like it better.

"The main difference we see between the groups is motivation—the children in the video game group enjoy the sessions more, and it's easier for parents to get them to come to our clinic," said Olafur Palsson, Ph.D., of Eastern Virginia Medical School in Richmond, a co-inventor of the NASA system.

It may also encourage children to play G-rated video games, which work best with the system, says Lindsay Greco, a vice president at CyberLearning Technologies. "The games that don't work well are the shoot-'em-up, blood-and-guts kind, because there is poor forward motion," says Greco. Games that involve steady motion, like driving a car or flying an airplane, work best.

For more information, log on to smartbraingames.com.

EVALUATING THE AUTHOR'S ARGUMENTS:

Much of the information in Rick Hodges's viewpoint comes from manufacturers who make the games designed to help kids with attention deficit disorder. Do these experts seem like knowledgeable, credible sources, or do you think their answers may be affected by their need to sell their companies' products? Explain your answer.

Chapter 3

Do Video Games Portray Minorities Fairly?

Many feel that games that portray racial stereotypes reinforce or introduce racial prejudice to children.

Viewpoint 1

Video Games Are Becoming More Gay-Friendly

"The general trend in gaming . . . is toward more honest and realistic representations of people in all their diversity."

Alice Bonasio

In the following article Alice Bonasio argues that video games are becoming more gay-friendly. Video games and the industry itself have a history of being homophobic, she writes, but gradually designers have been trying to cater to a more diverse audience by adding elements such as gay characters and same-sex marriages and by giving players options to make choices about their characters' sexual preferences. Bonasio argues that although there are still remnants of the old macho gaming culture, the general trend is toward more inclusive and diverse games. Bonasio is a British journalist who covers video games.

AS YOU READ, CONSIDER THE FOLLOWING QUESTIONS:

1. Why were most games made for white, heterosexual males in the game industry's infancy, according to the article?
2. List two video game franchises that have been praised for being gay-friendly, as cited by the author.
3. What part of *Grand Theft Auto IV* is considered to be a positive example for gay content, according to Bonasio?

Alice Bonasio, "Straight and Narrow," *The Escapist Magazine,* October 6, 2009. Reproduced by permission.

After a few minutes on Xbox Live [an online multiplayer gaming service], you're likely to be convinced that the gaming community is rabidly homophobic. The frequency with which players casually fling around words like "fag," "homo" and "gay" as insults is enough to deter all but the most thick-skinned gay gamers from joining in the fun. But there's a more subtle bias against homosexuality that's long been the norm in the games industry: the near absence of gay characters in single-player games.

It's an issue that has come into greater focus as videogames have aspired to tell more complex stories with more nuanced characters. But despite these goals, the experiences that designers have created for players are too often limited to a heterosexual male perspective. It's a double-edged sword: Designers are reluctant to include homosexuality in their games because many people would object to being forced to play a gay character. Flip that issue around, though, and you realize how unfair this is to gay gamers, who must play as heterosexual characters if they want to play at all.

"I can't recall off the top of my head any games that blatantly expressed homophobic comments or ideals. But the fact that there were no games depicting gays was a milder form of silent homophobia that the industry suffered from as a whole," says George Skleres, a game designer who happens to be gay. "It definitely sends a message to people who play a lot of games that 'normalcy' is being white and heterosexual, because the hero is always white and heterosexual."

A History of Homophobia

Chris Vizzini, founder of gaymer.org, echoes Skleres' sentiments. "I would like to have the option to choose to be a gay character and have it smoothly integrate into the storyline," he says. "We just want to be included without ridicule."

Unfortunately, such characters are a rarity. When games do feature gay characters, it's often in a harmful light. "Sometimes we are negatively stereotyped," says Vizzini. "Case and point would be *Grand Theft Auto: Vice City*. There is a guy depicted as a swishy queen roller-skating down the street in hot pants and leg warmers. No one I know is like that."

This lack of sensitivity is partly due to the lack of openly gay developers at most studios. "The game industry in its infancy was very homophobic. It's not that gay people weren't employed, but the anti-gay tendencies that permeated the industry kept most of them in the closet," Skleres says. "For a long time, because the developers were primarily white, heterosexual men, the games were made for white, heterosexual men. Anyone outside of the 18-to-25 male demographic was completely untapped."

Slowly, though, it seems that developers are acknowledging the existence of the gay gamer audience by introducing homosexual paths, mainly in sandbox games. In open-world games, the responsibility for exploring these options lies with the player, which makes them a natural starting point for developers to acknowledge homosexuality without forcing it on players. The Sims and Fable franchises have long been praised for their gay-friendliness, but allowing gay relationships can still be controversial; *Bully* was attacked for featuring the option for the main character to kiss other boys.

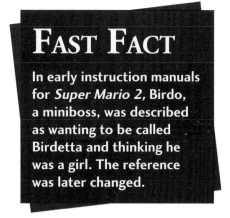

FAST FACT

In early instruction manuals for *Super Mario 2*, Birdo, a miniboss, was described as wanting to be called Birdetta and thinking he was a girl. The reference was later changed.

For games industry giant and Fable creator Peter Molyneux, the inclusion of gay characters and relationship options in his games was a non-issue. "Adult sexual preference is part of the choice of who you are and what you want to experiment with. That fitted perfectly with what *Fable II* was and so enhanced the gameplay."

"*Fable II* is a game which allows people to be themselves," Molyneux continues. "For me, as a designer, it was not a case of 'should we include this feature?' as it was obvious that we should include it. It was a very natural process, as we felt you should be able to flirt with any consenting adult of either the same sex or the opposite sex. There was never any debate about this; we just felt it was a natural part of creating a world. The key thing here is to offer the player the choice."

The Industry Is Becoming More Inclusive

Vizzini says the best games don't turn the gay options into a huge deal. He cites *Sims 2* as a brilliant example of this, because it allowed two men or two women to get together as a matter of course; homosexual choices

According to Peter Molyneux (pictured), creator of Fable II, *"Adult sexual preferences are part of the choice of who you are" and are included in the game to enhance game play.*

did not affect the rules of the game one way or another. "Unlike in real life, you could get married or have kids. It was great!" Vizzini enthuses. "You better believe there was an Eric and Chris couple shacked up in a 5,000-square-foot mansion."

"I think the inclusion of same-sex relationships and marriage in *The Sims* and *Fable II* shows the industry is becoming more inclusive," says Skleres. "The player is free to create their own story and their character's sexuality by the choices they make. But I wouldn't go so far as to say we have a positive representation of homosexuality—I have yet to see a game with a developer-designed, openly gay protagonist."

That doesn't mean designers have shied away from gay NPCs [non-player characters] and supporting characters, however. Skleres cites *Grand Theft Auto IV* as a positive example: "There is a mission you have to undertake to save Florian, an openly gay character, from a homophobe that keeps harassing him in the park when he is running. I am really proud of Rockstar Games for including this content in their game. It shows that even bad-ass mercenary hitmen can be tolerant and supportive of gays. Not only that, but the next episode in their series is titled *The Ballad of Gay Tony*, which should prove to be interesting."

For Molyneux, the future of game design will inevitably be more diverse and inclusive. "The better we get at making games, the more opportunities there are to feature more characters from different backgrounds and cultures. Most of the characters in games up until recently have been very iconic—the iconic hero, the iconic villain and the iconic victim—and it's only now we can add many more aspects and personality to those characters," he says.

The Trend Is Toward Diversity

Skleres argues that bringing new perspectives into the development process will have a big impact on the types of games the industry produces. "Overall, I think the industry has matured enough to where everyone recognizes having a diverse team can only help make a better product," he says. "Entertainment professionals put into their creations a bit of their own personal experiences and beliefs whether they realize it or not. As a result, when you get a more diverse set of professionals, their experiences and beliefs diversify too."

"There are still echoing remnants of the 'macho' culture left, but companies are no longer putting up with the testosterone-overloaded work environment that used to dominate the industry," says Skleres. "They want to maximize their human resources and tap into demographic markets that aren't typical mainstream gamers, and to do this they need game creators that can think like their target audience."

While Skleres and Vizzini have both made a place for themselves in the industry and the gamer community, respectively, there are still problems to confront and barriers to break down. Every minority that does not fit the white-male-heterosexual mold has had to claw and bite its way toward acceptance and representation, and gay gamers are no exception. The general trend in gaming, however, is toward more honest and realistic representations of people in all their diversity, which makes gay developers and players alike more optimistic about the future.

"The perception of a macho culture in the games industry is slowly dwindling and will probably fade away entirely in the near future. I'm glad games are growing up," says Skleres. Hopefully we'll soon be enjoying games where all races, creeds, genders and sexual orientations are represented, and not just as token gestures or caricatures. For gay gamers, that time can't come soon enough.

> **EVALUATING THE AUTHOR'S ARGUMENTS:**
>
> In this viewpoint Alice Bonasio relies heavily on experts to make her points for her. Do you think this is a more effective technique than if she had simply made the points herself? Why or why not?

Video Games Are Becoming Less Gay-Friendly

"Once again gay characters are treated as the villains and the comic relief."

Brad Hilderbrand

In the following article Brad Hilderbrand argues that video games are regressing and becoming less gay-friendly. He notes that there was a more thoughtful and sensitive approach to gay characters during a so-called "Golden Age" in the early 2000s, but games now are reverting to their old stereoptypes. He criticizes the video game industry for lagging behind television and cinema in the treatment of gay issues and for playing it safe, "putting sales above message." Hilderbrand is cohost of the Kombo Breaker Team podcast.

AS YOU READ, CONSIDER THE FOLLOWING QUESTIONS:

1. What is the sidequest, or extra task, from *Fable II* that inspired Hilderbrand to write this essay?
2. Name three video game characters the author lists as portraying gay people in a "negative and stereotypical light."
3. What game features a character whose gender was changed for American audiences because he kisses another male character, according to the author?

Who would have thought that it would take an optional mission in a random game to get me thinking about the state of homosexual characters in today's games, but it seems that's precisely what happened. You see, the other day I was tromping about in *Fable II* when I happened across a random farm in the countryside. Like most regions in *Fable*, the kindly proprietor of the farm had a task for me, one which I took on with much relish. You see, the farmer was concerned about his son, a strapping young man who had yet to find that special lady with whom he would carry on the family name. Our friend of the earth asked me to go into the city and find a proper date for his boy, a gal who could make the surprisingly eligible bachelor happy. I took on the task, but figured it would be wise to chat with the young man first, as this all seemed a bit odd.

Sure enough, when I mentioned the task to the farmer's son he immediately got nervous and began to stumble and stammer. This boy had a secret, and I was beginning to understand exactly what it was. I decided to head off into town and woo a villager for this lovelorn soul, and I did exactly that, and he was a fine gentleman indeed. That's right, though the random NPC [nonplayer character] in the sidequest [an extra task a player may perform] never said the words out loud, the boy was gay, and he had been trapped living a lie for a long, long time.

After finding the date and returning to the farm, I witnessed what was a rather tender moment between father and son, as the boy opened up to his dad about his hidden feelings and his father reacted first with genuine shock, then acceptance and understanding. While it may be the sort of outing homosexual individuals hope for when they finally decide to break the news, things rarely work out so calmly. All in all, it was a surprisingly touching moment for a game which up to that point had allowed me to wantonly kill villagers; loot and

> ## Fast Fact
>
> Twenty-seven percent of parents found video game images of two men kissing to be offensive versus 25 percent who were offended by images of a graphically severed head, according to a 2008 survey by the Web site WhatTheyPlay.

pillage till my pockets were overflowing; and generally be all sorts of a bastard. I had never expected *Fable* to teach me a lesson in matters of human sexuality, and it got me thinking.

After finishing up the quest I immediately put the game down and began to think. Had I ever seen the issue of homosexuality handled so delicately in a game before? My mind raced for examples of past gay characters, and the figures I settled on didn't exactly paint a flattering picture. The first individual that sprang to mind was Makoto from the JRPG [Japanese role-playing game] *Enchanted Arms*. Anyone who has played this game knows that dear sweet Makoto isn't exactly the person GLAAD [Gay and Lesbian Alliance Against Defamation] is going to be putting at the front of the parade in order to dispel homosexual stereotypes. He is as flamboyant a character as can be, and his appearance in a game alone like[ly] set the gay rights movement back at least 20 years where gaming is concerned. The sad thing was, as I kept searching for more examples things didn't get much better; Mr. Silver and Mr. Gold from *God Hand*, Roxy and Poison from *Final Fight*, even our old pal Birdo from *Super Mario Bros*, all of them portray gay characters in a negative and stereotypical light. So the question becomes, is it time for the gaming industry to join television and films in the more sensitive portrayal of these characters, or is the medium simply not ready for such sweeping change?

The History of Gay Characters

In order to understand where we are now, it becomes necessary to look back at the history of gaming and see how far we have come. Since nearly the beginning of gaming gay characters have been utilized, though they almost always fell under the categories of villain or comic foil. These early characters were often cross-dressing, effeminate individuals whose inclusion as comic relief helped them circumvent Nintendo and Sega's censorship codes, which were modeled off the early Hollywood production codes which banned "sexual perversion." Also, the late 80s and early 90s marked the height of the AIDS scare, when many Americans first became aware of the disease and associated [it] almost exclusively with members of the homosexual community. This vilification of the entire group seeped into gaming as well, as the lifestyle was decried as "evil" by many in the mainstream community.

As times changed the portrayal of gay characters softened, and by the mid-90s and at the turn of the millennium, homosexual characters were being treated with a bit more tact. There were still plenty of the old stereotyped characters to go around, but games like *Indigo Prophecy: The Longest Journey* and *Metal Gear Solid 2* and *3* all featured openly gay or bisexual characters and gave them more to do than prance about in women's clothing speaking with a lisp and getting into slap fights. 2001 was also the year the original *Fable* was released, giving players the opportunity to date and marry same-sex partners if they so chose. For many, this was the first time in gaming where they could actually control their own romantic destiny rather than being led toward a simple and inevitable conclusion with one specific character, and the reactions varied widely from interest and intrigue to downright disgust.

It's no surprise that the earlier part of this decade was a sort of "Golden Age" for gay game characters; it was also the time other segments of the media began to treat the lifestyle with a more thoughtful approach. This was largely due to the emergence of *Will & Grace* as a television hit, and later years brought the success of *Queer Eye for the Straight Guy* and the advent of "metrosexualism." Furthermore, 2006's *Brokeback Mountain* brought the trials and tribulations of a gay relationship into mainstream cinema (yes, there have been mov-

The Metal Gear Solid series of video games has been one of the few games to portray gay characters in a positive manner.

Gay Gamers on Homophobia in Games

- **Fifty-three percent think the gaming community is "somewhat hostile" to gay and lesbian gamers.**

- **Fourteen percent think the gaming community is "very hostile" to gay and lesbian gamers.**

- **Eighty-seven percent had encountered the phrase "that's so gay" while gaming.**

- **Fifty-two percent thought stereotypical representations of gay characters was homophobic.**

- **Forty-three percent thought the "refusal of game designers to include well-developed gay characters" was homophobic.**

Taken from: James Rockwell, "Gaymer Survey," 2007. http://gaygamer.net.

ies with gay characters for a long time; no, most people didn't notice or care until *Brokeback*), cementing the issue at the forefront of the social agenda. As society goes, so goes gaming, and this was the period when a sort of "Gay Renaissance" struck the landscape.

Games Falling Back onto Stereotypes

These periods of change don't last forever, though, and as the issue has receded in the public eye, games have reverted back to previous stereotypes once thought to be on the way out. Once again gay characters are treated as the villains and the comic relief, with Makoto being but one example of how far we have fallen. Something fans might not know is that the game *Paper Mario: The Thousand Year Door* actually features a character whose gender was changed for the sake of American audiences. Vivian, one of the Shadow Sisters, appears as a male character in the Japanese version of the game, but due to a scene in which (s)he kisses Mario on the cheek and expresses feelings for the protagonist Nintendo chose to change the character's gender for American audiences in order to avoid controversy.

Thus, even though we saw a glimpse of equality a few years ago, unfortunately games have fallen back into the rut of stereotype and hyperbole. While there are brief moments in games like *Fable II* or *Metal Gear Solid* that treat homosexuality with a careful, thoughtful approach, the game industry seems to be far more comfortable sticking with tired clichés and stereotypes for the sake of not offending, but also not progressing. Unfortunately, in a market where [video game character] Marcus Fenix stands as the definition of a man and [character] Lara Croft is the essence of what it means to be a woman, there seems to be little inclination to tackle one of society's biggest taboos. While games have the potential to stand at the bleeding edge of social and political commentary, they prefer to play it safe and put sales above message, lagging far behind their contemporaries in television and cinema. Games simply refuse to be gay, and for that we all suffer.

EVALUATING THE AUTHOR'S ARGUMENTS:

Brad Hilderbrand makes no reference to whether he is gay. Is this fact important to the argument or is it irrelevant? For someone to write about discrimination, must they be part of the group enduring discrimination? Explain your answer.

Games for Girls May Simply Reflect What Girls Like

"As ridiculous as we may find them, these games [for girls] accurately represent the interests of a segment of the population."

Susan Arendt

In the following selection Susan Arendt argues that it is pointless to criticize video games designed for girls as "shoehorning girls into stereotypes." Girls, she writes, already like such things as boys, make up, and fashion—the games are simply reflecting those interests. The problem is not that these sorts of games exist, she argues, it is the lack of alternatives to these kinds of games. Arendt is a senior editor for the *Escapist*.

AS YOU READ, CONSIDER THE FOLLOWING QUESTIONS:
1. What are a few of the interest areas that the author claims are not negative stereotypes but are instead accurate reflections of what young girls like?
2. List three strong female protagonists the author mentions.
3. What solution does the author suggest that would allow girls more choice in choosing video game characters?

Susan Arendt, "Silly Girls," *The Escapist Magazine*, July 16, 2009. Reproduced by permission.

Game Life's talented Tracey John recently took a look at the life lessons to be learned from "tween" girl games, and though her article was meant to be tongue-in-cheek, many used it as a springboard to hurl invective at the idea of games directed at a female audience. Forums lit up with declarations that "I'm a girl and I play [fill in name of bloody/violent/testosterone-filled game here]!!" and there was much wailing and crying about shoehorning girls into stereotypes.

Seriously, people, calm the hell down.

For starters, what's the real danger, here? Are we really saying that playing *Chinatown Wars* won't inspire a girl to pursue a career in drug trafficking but somehow playing *Top Model* will forever doom her to a life of low self-esteem and bulimia? Sorry, folks, but you don't get to have it both ways; either videogames directly influence your behavior and choices, or they don't. Unless you want to start saying that yeah, maybe playing first person shooters really does help turn kids into killers, you don't get to voice concern about the negative impact that *Princess in Love* might have on your niece.

Ah, what's that I hear? That these games "perpetuate negative stereotypes"? Which stereotypes would these be, exactly? The ones that young girls like cute boys, looking at clothes, and gossiping about each other? Granted, it's been a few years since I was the target demographic for these games, but when I was a wee lass, I engaged in all of those activities so much that I practically had Master's Degrees in them. I somewhat doubt all that much has changed.

The simple truth is that young girls like stupid things. They like shopping and makeup and boys and ponies and glitter and The Jonas Brothers and a whole legion of other things that will make you feel like your brain is dissolving if you think about them for too long. And please, this is not your cue to protest about how you were never like that, you liked bugs and science and all the things that small girls typically don't because you're not about to be forced into some label, dammit! Get over it. If you grew up preferring dirtbikes to Barbies, that's grand, but if you didn't—if you fretted over the best color nail polish and prowled the local clothing stores like a lion on the savannah—well, that's ok, too.

It Is Not Wrong to Be Girly

There seems to be some kind of prevailing idea that being a silly little girl is somehow intrinsically *wrong* and that games that treat females as such are committing some kind of social evil. This is, simply put, bullshit. Though we may prefer for our young ladies to be serious-minded intellectuals or at the very least scorching nerds, not all of them are. As ridiculous as we may find them, these games accurately represent the interests of a segment of the population. The problem isn't that we're telling girls they can go shopping, find boyfriends, or design jewelry—the problem is we're not telling them much of anything *else*.

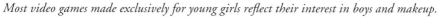

Most video games made exclusively for young girls reflect their interest in boys and makeup.

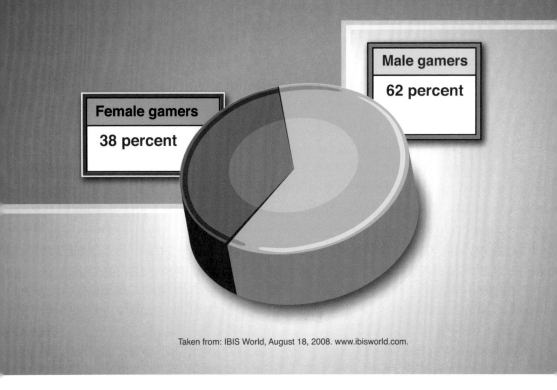

Girls Make Up a Big Part of the Video Game Market

Male gamers

62 percent

Female gamers

38 percent

Taken from: IBIS World, August 18, 2008. www.ibisworld.com.

It would be wonderful to see *Science Mama* alongside *Cooking Mama* in the store, but we apparently have to leave that sort of thing to Papa. Great message being sent there, gang. Boys get to be wizards, detectives, and heroes. Girls get to be princesses.

I'm not going to be so daring as to ask for more female protagonists, more Samuses and Laras and Jades. I mean, there's no reason why Gordon Freeman had to be a guy, after all, he could've just as easily been Brenda Freeman, but that's a debate for a different day. And honestly, that would just trade the current inadequate system for a new and differently inadequate one. An overabundance of games with female leads is no better than our current situation, in which everyone saving the world has a five o'clock shadow. Well, the humans, anyway. For now, I'd settle for more games in which the main character's gender is left up to the player's personal preference. What could be more fair? Why does Sora have to be a boy? Why can't the Elite Beat Agents be girls? I don't want to hear about how that mucks around with the storyline, either, because *Mass Effect* and *Fable 2* both pulled it off just fine.

Let's stop blaming so-called "girl" games for what isn't their fault—the fact that videogames continue to fail at painting a variety of pictures when it comes to female characters. Girls can be many things—warriors, mothers, soldiers, scientists, and yes, fashion designers—but you'd never know that by looking at the videogame landscape. Let's deal with that before focusing too much of our attention on the possible long-term effects of playing *Style Savvy*.

EVALUATING THE AUTHOR'S ARGUMENTS:

Susan Arendt peppers her argument with very informal language. Does this affect how you read the argument or view the author's credibility? Explain your answer.

Viewpoint
4

"*Most video games for girls send a steady flow of narrow images and self-limiting notions about how to succeed in today's culture.*"

Games for Girls Perpetuate Negative Stereotypes

Michael Abbott

In this selection Michael Abbott argues that games designed for girls reinforce old and tired ideas about what a girl needs to succeed in the world. Games about being popular, beautiful, and fashionable may have a place in the game world, he argues, but they should not form the entire girls' market. Abbott, a parent of a small girl, cautions that parents need to worry about the kinds of messages these games are sending to girls. Abbott is the creator of the Brainy Gamer, a blog and podcast.

AS YOU READ, CONSIDER THE FOLLOWING QUESTIONS:
1. List a few of what the author calls "essentialist tropes" for girls.
2. According to Abbott, in the game *Drama Queens*, can players get in a catfight to see who is the most popular diva?
3. Name three games designed for girls mentioned in the article.

Michael Abbott, "OMG, Girls in Trouble!" The Brainy Gamer, May 13, 2009. Reproduced by permission.

I talk to a lot of parents about video games, and many of them continue to worry about the negative effects of games on their kids. If you dig a little deeper in these conversations, you quickly discover their concerns have little to do with their daughters. It's the boys they're worried about. When I say "video game" they hear "violent killing game," and they fear the messages these games send to their impressionable sons.

They should worry more about their daughters.

Most video games for girls send a steady flow of narrow images and self-limiting notions about how to succeed in today's culture. They reinforce all the worn-out essentialist tropes [the idea that all members of a certain group will share the same characteristics]: be beautiful, be

FAST FACT

Topics for so-called "girl games" at the games Web site GamesGames include cooking, makeup, nail fashion, dress up, dating, and caring.

In a departure from the stereotypical games designed for girls, video-game maker Ubisoft produces a line of games featuring dancing, gymnastics, and horse riding.

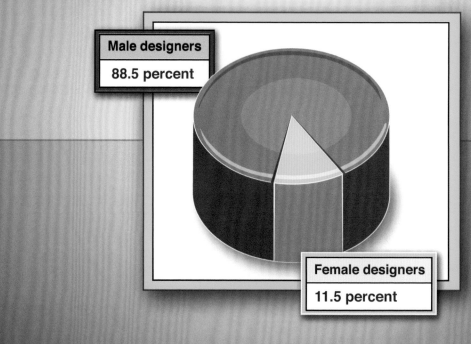

Women Are Still a Minority of Game Designers

Male designers

88.5 percent

Female designers

11.5 percent

Taken from: International Game Developers Association, 2005.

fashionable, be popular. If parents want to worry about the messages kids receive from video games, they should pay more attention to these. The "dangerous" M-rated games that provoke all the parental hand-wringing are intended for adults. A game like *Drama Queens* (Majesco) is targeted and marketed directly to young teenage girls.

I'll let Majesco's marketing speak for itself:

- Chelsi stole my boyfriend but Hayden is totally crushing on me—must be because of the little black dress I bought after landing a promotion at Fashion Boutique. Step aside, ladies!
- Play a fierce cat fight to see who is the most popular queen diva.
- Play in four environments from the shopping mall to the fashion runway.
- Show up to three friends that you're most popular in two multiplayer modes.

Search for games designed for girls, and you'll discover that *Drama Queens* isn't exactly operating on the outer fringe. *Style Up for Wedding; Style Up for Prom; Hair Stylin Salon; Bratz Makeover Game; Sue Hairdresser; Lovely in Pink; Bride and Groom; Nail Art Salon* . . . they're mostly online games, and they go on and on and on just like this. Sure, there's probably a place for such games, but in the "games for girls" market, it's pretty much the only place.

Games for Girls Lack Subtlety

If a boy gets his hands on *Gears of War 2* or *Call of Duty 4*, he'll see things his parents may not want him to see; but he may also be exposed to a series of messages expressing ambivalence about violence and pondering the devastation of war. I'm not suggesting 12-year-olds play these games, nor do I think these games function as anti-war treatises. But they at least reflect, if only cursorily, on some thought-provoking themes. Ironically, the game genre parents find most troubling is the very genre most likely to contain thematically subtle content these days (see also *Far Cry 2*).

It's hard to find anything subtle in the little pink games made for girls by mostly male developers. *Drama Queens* and dozens of other similar games for girls are gameplay renderings of self-absorbed consumerism. As a parent of a small girl, I think I'd rather let her play *Far Cry 2* when she's 13 (and discuss it with me) than to de-program her from the cultural brainwashing of a game like *Drama Queens*.

> **EVALUATING THE AUTHOR'S ARGUMENTS:**
>
> Before reading Michael Abbott's article, did you have an opinion about video games made for girls? Did his arguments affect how you looked at the issue? Why or why not?

Games Are Unfairly Labeled as Racist

"Games with minority characters, and especially minority stereotypes— even tongue-in-cheek characters not meant to be offensive— are torn down by accusations of intolerance."

Chris Mottes

In the following viewpoint Chris Mottes argues that video games and video game developers are unfairly singled out for being racist. It is a double standard, he writes, when other media, such as film, television, and literature, are applauded for portraying morally ambiguous, racist characters but video games are condemned for the same thing. This unfounded criticism, he argues, leads to self-censorship and limits artistic expression. Mottes is the chief executive officer of Deadline Games.

AS YOU READ, CONSIDER THE FOLLOWING QUESTIONS:
1. List two of the efforts the author's company made to ensure an accurate Mexican feel for the games *Total Overdose* and *Chili Con Carnage.*
2. What other forms of media, according to the author, are freer to include racist and morally gray characters?
3. What two things, according to Mottes, motivate developers toward self-censorship?

Members of the media often attack video games for being racist, sexist, mean-spirited, callous, unpleasant, insensitive, or just generally nasty. As a developer, I find most of these claims not only a touch insulting but also extremely tenuous, and in the majority of cases unfounded.

More than a few titles in recent memory have drawn rather incensed reactions from critics over plotlines, characters, jokes, or even gameplay characteristics they deemed inappropriate. Names like Hillary Clinton, Jack Thompson, and Dr. Phil top the list of knee-jerk reactionaries on the subject of tastelessness in video games. Pundits generally set their sights on the two big evils: sex and violence.

But while critics most frequently assert that video games contain too much violence and sex, they also endeavor to expose games as racially prejudiced. Games with minority characters, and *especially* minority stereotypes—even tongue-in-cheek characters not meant to be offensive—are torn down by accusations of intolerance. A surprising number of critics condemn video games as blatantly racist, and we're not merely talking about mainstream celebrities. We're talking about game reviewers and other members of the enthusiast media. We're talking about an astonishing majority of online columnists, bloggers, and forum posters who persistently speak out against any game that contains what they believe to be racial stereotyping.

Unfair Criticism

Total Overdose and *Chili Con Carnage,* titles I helped develop at Deadline Games, were both targets of this type of criticism. When we designed these games, our goal was to provide a well-rounded,

"Videogame Employment Agency," cartoon by Stuart Harrison, www.CartoonStock.com. © Stuart Harrison. Reproduction rights obtainable from www.CartoonStock.com.

entertaining experience on many levels. We wanted exciting gameplay, but we were just as interested in having a compelling story, cast of characters, and setting, which is why we invested a great deal of energy towards researching the culture of Mexico, so we could produce an experience that was drawn from accurate source material.

When researching for *Total Overdose*, we spent a great deal of time in Mexico, taking over 6,000 photos—photos that were the basis for the vast majority of the textures that appeared in the game. We visited a variety of nightclubs to influence the settings and humor of the game, and we spent time in the company of self-styled gangsters to get a flavor for how they spoke and what they said.

When recording dialogue for both games, we employed Mexican-American voice actors to ensure that we would be providing accurate representations. And when it was time to decide on the soundtrack, we chose to include music from several acclaimed underground Mexican bands, including Molotov, who enjoyed the game to such a great extent that they offered to record unique tunes for a sequel.

However, in reviews, forums, and blogs following the releases of both games, some people slammed Deadline for being bigoted towards Mexicans. While we did employ stereotypes we considered lighthearted and humorous, our intent was most certainly *not* to cast Mexican individuals in a derogatory light. In fact, we continue to receive fan mail from Mexican gamers who love the games and praise us for depicting our cartoon version of Mexico as a modern, if corrupt, place.

But despite our best efforts, critics still slammed us for being racists. I have to wonder why [director] Robert Rodriguez movies—films to which our games have been regularly compared—are spared this same kind of criticism.

Many other games have received similar criticism from the media. One of the major titles that went through this was *Grand Theft Auto: Vice City. Vice City* received high-profile criticism for an out-of-context line of dialogue: "Kill all the Haitians!" The quote was taken from a sequence that pitted the player against a Haitian drug-pushing gang. The developers were not promoting violence against all Haitians, or even insinuating that all Haitians are violent drug dealers. Clearly, the game contains blatantly racist characters. But does that make the game itself, and the game's developers, racists themselves?

> **FAST FACT**
>
> In a 2009 study of minority video game characters by the University of Southern California Annenberg School for Communication, less that 3 percent were found to be Latino, and of those, all were nonspeaking background characters.

A Double Standard

There exists a double standard.

The first line of dialogue in the 2006 movie *The Departed*, spoken by [actor] Jack Nicholson's character, derides black people in a vulgar and insulting manner. Why can [director] Martin Scorsese get away with including racist, morally grey characters in his movies? Why can movies, music, television, theatre, and literature get away with it? These media receive significantly less criticism when they portray racist characters—even racist, morally questionable protagonists. Is it simply because video games are an

Some video game designers contend that if it is acceptable for Hollywood to use racial stereotypes, then the same should hold true for video games.

interactive form of entertainment? If that's the argument, I think it's an evasive one.

The constant criticism and threat of legal action motivates developers towards self-censorship. In my opinion, this is an awful consequence. Artistic expression is not limited to traditional forms of media. Interactive art is still art. And most everyone can agree that censorship, by and large, is a *bad* thing. In the end, games are only as strong as the vision of their developers, and when we begin to question ourselves, the final result suffers dramatically.

We need to demolish the double standard. Racism is a terrible, awful thing; there is no doubt about that. And while games that are patently, intentionally racist do exist, most games with racist characters *do not* reflect the mindset of their developers. Strictly good and evil characters do not populate the best stories. The best stories contain dynamic characters that exist in a continuum of moral right and wrong. And if a character possesses qualities that lean mostly into the "wrong" column, that should not be interpreted as a representation of the world view of that character's creator.

This conclusion is widely accepted when considering other forms of entertainment. Why are video games an exception?

EVALUATING THE AUTHOR'S ARGUMENTS:

In this viewpoint Chris Mottes details his company's efforts to create an authentic Mexican feel for his games. Do you think these efforts negate claims that the games are racist? Do you agree that video games as an artistic media are unfairly singled out for being racist? Explain.

Viewpoint
6

Racist Stereotypes in Games Reinforce Racist Attitudes

Richard O. Jones

"One of the side effects of playing such [racist] video games for long periods of time is that the anti-productive images are mentally implanted."

In the following selection Richard O. Jones argues that video games reinforce racist stereotypes. When black characters are primarily victims or criminals, he argues, these depictions send a harmful message to minority children. And because black children are the biggest consumers of video games, they are the most affected by these kinds of stereotypes. The solution to a fairer portrayal of minorities, according to Jones, is for minority children who love video games to channel that energy into learning how to design games. Jones is a comedian and a writer for the *Black Voice News* Web site.

Richard O. Jones, "The Bad News and Good News of Obsessive Video Games, Parts 1 and 2," *Black VoiceNews.com,* February 8, 2007. Reproduced by permission.

AS YOU READ, CONSIDER THE FOLLOWING QUESTIONS:
1. What percentage of video game developers are black, according to the International Game Developers Association study cited by the author?
2. According to the Kaiser Family Foundation study cited in the article, which group of teen boys played more video games?
3. Which demographic group was most likely to be a victim of violence in a game, according to the Children Now study cited in the article?

Negative video games reinforce poor self-images in Black youth. One of the side effects of playing such video games for long periods of time is that the anti-productive images are mentally implanted. In the popular video game *Grand Theft Auto: San Andreas*, players assume the lead character of Carl Johnson, a down-on-his-luck Black criminal who roams city streets stealing cars and helping gang members knock off rivals in drive-by shootings.

Recently, I watched a DVD with two 12-year-old boys. The movie was called *Inside Man* starring Denzel Washington. There is a small segment of the movie where a young Black boy is playing a hand-held video game. In the game there are Blacks shooting Blacks. The wall and street is spattered with blood. Both of the boys I watched the movie with found that segment exciting. I'm glad I witnessed their reaction. I plan to discus the subject with both. Psychologists agree that if your race is always the thief or killer, then after a while you start to think that's how you should be, or you think that's how your people are.

FAST FACT

The first obviously black video game character appeared in the 1979 Atari game *Basketball*.

"If Blacks and Latinos are always portrayed as the villains, or as the victims who get killed often and easily, that is code for powerlessness," said Kansas State University psychologist John Murray, who's studied violence and stereotypes in the media for the past 30 years.

These images persist because too few minorities are in the industry. Roughly 80% of video game programmers are white, about four percent of designers are Latino, and less than three percent are Black according to preliminary results of an International Game Developers Association survey. Some in the industry believe race in games is a serious issue that has been ignored for too long. The video industry claims that educated, young white males create games for other educated, young white males and not minorities.

Regardless, games are an expressive medium. They are an art form, just like movies, theater and literature. We're seeing, to a large extent, that the games that are being designed unconsciously include the biases, opinions and reflections of their creators. And obviously, whites see Blacks and Latinos as criminals and gradually that's how our children see themselves and behave accordingly. A 2006 study by the Kaiser Family Foundation revealed that Black youths between 8 and 18 years old played video and computer games roughly 90 minutes a day—almost 30 minutes more than white youths. And Latinos play about 10 minutes more per day than whites. Therefore, since Blacks

Experts say that black children, who are the biggest consumers of video games, are negatively affected by stereotyped portrayals in many games of black people as criminals.

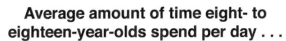

Differences in Media Use by Race

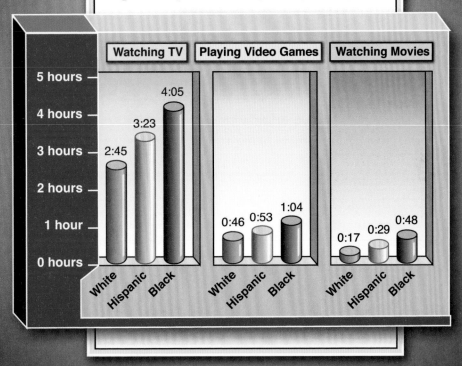

Average amount of time eight- to eighteen-year-olds spend per day . . .

| Watching TV | Playing Video Games | Watching Movies |

White: 2:45, Hispanic: 3:23, Black: 4:05 (Watching TV)

White: 0:46, Hispanic: 0:53, Black: 1:04 (Playing Video Games)

White: 0:17, Hispanic: 0:29, Black: 0:48 (Watching Movies)

Taken from: Kaiser Family Foundation, "Generation M: Media in the Lives of 8—18 Year-Olds," March 2005.

are the most obsessive players it stands to reason that Blacks are the most negatively affected. However, experts say that if you've got kids who can sit in front of a video game for hours, then they have the cognitive thought process to learn how to build the game.

The Industry Needs More Minorities

The video game industry is all about money. No one really cares about your skin color or gender if you are a well-trained video game designer or illustrator. The problem is that our youth and adult players see themselves as players and not designers or illustrators.

Therefore unless they're motivated to get on the business end versus the player end of the video game phenomenon they will continue to be portrayed in a negative light and also miss out on a ten billion dollar a year industry.

I have adult males in my family, well into their 30s and early 40s, that are as addicted to playing video games as teenage boys. They enjoy playing against an opponent who is sitting somewhere in another location, perhaps another state, and they are connected electronically. During the Christmas season, I remember seeing young men sleeping outside of stores in order to assure that they didn't miss an opportunity to purchase a new upgraded version of some type of video game player or entertainment center. There were even reports of fistfights and customers being robbed at gunpoint for their cherished purchase.

If these crazed players would spend a portion of their life learning to create these games instead of wasting their lives playing them there would be as many Black millionaire video game designers and illustrators as there is athletes and music artists. Parents and wives should redirect the video players of their household into thinking about being trained to earn money from their passion. They could also be the force that stops the negative images of Blacks and women in video games.

In a study of some of the most popular video games—both "console" games, like Nintendo and PlayStation, and the increasingly common computer-based "PC" games—the advocacy group "Children Now" uncovered some startling statistics.

A Need for Positive Role Models

"African American females were far more likely to be victims of violence," said Eileen Espejo, senior program associate for Children Now's Children and the Media Program. "And African American characters in general were least likely to respond to pain," like bleeding or groaning. The study also found that characters in games for young children were exclusively white. "It's not representative of the world we live in," Espejo said. "Children Now" encourages video game developers to ask themselves whether their products create or exploit stereotypes and whether the content of their games is meaningful to children.

"We know that children need to see people like themselves in the media," Espejo said. "It makes them feel that people of their race are important, it gives them role models, and it tells kids that people of different backgrounds are . . . valuable."

Minority men and women with good math and science skills are prime candidates to enter the video industry job training programs as programmers. Those with art and computer skills make good designers and illustrators. Industry experts agree that designers and illustrators need to come from a more diverse walk of life in order to rid the video games of racist overtones. Presently, the video game industry is dominated by white educated males earning a six-figure income off grown men like my Black adult male relatives sitting at home playing with another player in another state.

EVALUATING THE AUTHOR'S ARGUMENTS:

In this selection Richard O. Jones argues that the best way to stop the negative stereotypes in video games is to get more minorities involved in the game industry. Do you think this is a good solution? Why or why not?

Facts About Video Games

Editor's note: These facts can be used in reports or papers to reinforce or add credibility when making important points or claims.

Video Games and Gamers

According to a 2009 Kaiser Family Foundation study:

- Ninety-seven percent of American teens play some type of video game. Ninety-nine percent of boys and 94 percent of girls play video games.
- Forty-eight percent of teens in grades seven to twelve say they text, listen to music, watch television, or use a computer while playing video games some or most of the time.
- The most popular games for teens are racing games, puzzles, and sports.
- Seventy-one percent of teens in grades seven to twelve have played *Rock Band* or *Guitar Hero.*
- Gamers spend an average of eighteen hours a week playing games.

According to the Entertainment Software Association:

- Fifty-three percent of American adults play video games.
- Forty percent of all game players are women.
- Fifty-seven percent of online gamers are male, and 43 percent are female.
- Women over the age of eighteen (34 percent) make up a bigger percentage of video game players than young men aged seventeen or younger (18 percent).
- The average age of a game player is thirty-nine.
- Twenty-five percent of people over age fifty play video games.
- Among adults sixty-five and older who play video games, nearly a third play every day.

The Business of Video Games
According to the NPD Group:

- Americans spent more than $20 billion on video game equipment in 2009.
- Total video game revenues now exceed box office and video rental revenues.
- Four of the top-five best sellers in 2009 were games for Nintendo's Wii system—*Wii Sports Resort, Wii New Mario Bros., Wii Fit,* and *Wii Fit Plus.*
- The top computer game of 2009 was *The Sims 3.*
- In 2008, 79.5 million video game software titles were sold.
- In 2009, 778 new video game software titles were released.
- Sixty-three percent of Americans have played a video game in the past six months, compared with 53 percent of people who have gone out to the movies.
- Video games make up one-third of the average monthly entertainment spending in the United States.

Call of Duty: Modern Warfare 2, the best-selling video game of 2009, has sold more than 11.86 million copies. The game has grossed more than $1 billion worldwide. In its first five days of release, the game earned $550 million, according to *Gamasutra.*

The price of *Call of Duty: Modern Warfare 2* is around fifty dollars on Amazon.

A top video game title can cost more than $100 million to make, according to National Public Radio.

It cost $30 million to make the top-selling game of 2007, *Halo 3,* according to DigitalSpy.com.

Video game programmers make an average of eighty-five thousand dollars a year. Entry-level junior game designers make an average of forty-six thousand dollars a year, according to Game Developer Research.

Jobs for computer software engineers are expected to grow by a third between 2010 and 2020, according to the Bureau of Labor Statistics.

Games and Society

According to a study by the Kaiser Family Foundation:

- Thirty-four percent of American teens have played a computer or video game at school as part of a school assignment.
- Thirty percent of kids report that their parents set rules about which video games they can play, 17 percent report their parents check warning labels or ratings on video games, and 12 percent report they play video games they know their parents do not want them playing.

According to a 2008 study by the Pew Internet and American Life Project:

- Thirty-two percent of teens aged twelve to sixteen play games that are listed as appropriate only for people older than they are.
- Thirty-two percent of gaming teens report that at least one of their favorite games is rated "Mature" or "Adults Only."
- Fifty-two percent of teen gamers report playing games where they think about moral and ethical issues.

According to a 2009 study by the University of Southern California Annenberg School for Communication:

- Game developers are 83.3 percent white, 7.5 percent Asian, 2.5 percent Latino, and 2.0 percent black.
- Game characters are approximately 59 percent white, 32 percent black, 2 percent Latino, 5 percent biracial, and less than 1 percent Asian. About 86 percent of characters are male and 14 percent are female.
- Kids use about 2 to 2.5 times more energy playing *Wii Bowling* and doing the beginner level of *Dance Dance Revolution* than they do watching television, according to a 2009 study in the journal *Pediatrics*.
- People who play massively multiplayer online role-playing games report more hours spent playing, worse health, worse sleep quality, and more problems with real-life socializing than people who play other types of video games, according to a 2009 study published in the journal *Computers in Human Behavior*.

Glossary

artificial intelligence (AI): The technology that allows nonplayer characters to react and behave realistically.

avatar: A video game user's physical representation or alter ego.

cybersickness: Motion sickness caused by playing a video game.

exergame: A video game that involves exercise.

gaymer: A gay, bisexual, or trangendered video game player.

massively multiplayer online role-playing game (MMORPG): A type of role-playing game in which a large number of people interact in a virtual world.

nonplayer character (NPC): A character whose actions are not controlled by the person playing the game.

role-playing game (RPG): A type of game in which players play as a character and interact with other players in a virtual world.

sidequest: An extra task in a game that is not directly related to the main goal. Sidequests may offer players a chance to earn special bonuses.

video game console: An interactive entertainment computer system designed solely to play video games on a television or monitor.

Organizations to Contact

The editors have compiled the following list of organizations concerned with the issues debated in this book. The descriptions are derived from materials provided by the organizations. All have publications or information available for interested readers. The list was compiled on the date of publication of the present volume; the information provided here may change. Be aware that many organizations take several weeks or longer to respond to inquiries, so allow as much time as possible for the receipt of requested materials.

Black Digerati
Web site: www.blackdigerati.org

Black Digerati is dedicated to promoting African Americans in digital technology, game development, and interactive media. The group works with industry and communities to provide opportunites and to increase interest among African Americans to work in these fields. The organization's Web site features news stories, videos, and profiles of successful African Americans in the industry.

Common Sense Media
650 Townsend St., Ste. 375, San Francisco, CA 94103
(415) 863-0600 • fax: (415) 863-0601
Web site: www.commonsensemedia.org

Common Sense Media is a nonprofit, nonpartisan organization with a mission of providing kids and families with information on media and technology. The group provides ratings of video games, Web sites, and music, among other forms of media, and offers articles for parents, educators, and kids. The group publishes the weekly *Common Sense Media Newsletter*.

EdgeGamers Organization
PMB 303
8414 Farm Rd., Ste. 180, Las Vegas, NV 89131-8171
Web site: www.edgegamers.org

The EdgeGamers Organization is dedicated to providing a safe place for gamers from all over the world to meet for family-friendly and respectful game play. Participants must follow a strict code of conduct that bans racist, political, and degrading speech. The organization's Web site offers an arcade, competitions, player blogs, news, and forums.

Edutopia
The George Lucas Educational Foundation
PO Box 3494, San Rafael, CA 94912
e-mail: info@edutopia.org
Web site: www.edutopia.org

Edutopia, a foundation run by the George Lucas Educational Foundation, is dedicated to increasing innovation—often through technology—in the educational system. The organization's Web site offers blogs, online groups, and special reports. The organization publishes the magazine *Edutopia*.

Entertainment Consumers Association (ECA)
64 Danbury Rd., Ste. 700, Wilton, CT 06897-4406
(203) 761-6180 • fax: (203) 761-6184
e-mail: feedback@theeca.com

The ECA is a nonprofit organization that advocates for the gaming community. The group lobbies against antigaming legislation and promotes the positive aspects of video games. The ECA publishes the nightly newsletter *ECA Today* and runs the GamePolitics Web site (www.gamepolitics.com).

Get-Well Gamers Foundation
21612 Hanakai Ln., Huntington Beach, CA 92646
(714) 963-1950
e-mail: getwellgamers@gmail.com
Web site: www.get-well-gamers.org

The Get-Well Gamers Foundation is an organization dedicated to providing video games and video game systems to children in hospitals. The group collects donations of money and equipment and distributes games and game systems to a network of more than eighty hospitals and treatment centers in the United States.

International Game Developers Association (IGDA)
Women in Games
e-mail: wigsig @ igda.org
Web site: http://archives.igda.org/women/

IGDA Women in Games is dedicated to supporting women in the video game industry. The organization hosts conferences and events, and its Web site has articles, job postings, and discussion groups. The group publishes the newsletter *IGDA Women in Games.*

On-Line Gamers Anonymous (OLGA) and OLG-Anon
104 Miller Ln., Harrisburg, PA 17110
OLGA/OLG-Anon hotline: (612) 245-1115
Web site: www.olganon.org

OLGA is a self-help fellowship for problem gamers and their families. The group offers a traditional twelve-step program and a modified program for atheists and agnostics. The organization's Web site has news, message boards, online meetings, reading lists, and information on finding professionals who work with problem gamers.

Parents' Choice Foundation
201 W. Padonia Rd., Ste. 303, Timonium, MD 21093
(410) 308-3858 • fax: (410) 308-3877
e-mail: info@parents-choice.org
Web site: www.parents-choice.org

The Parents' Choice Foundation is the nation's oldest nonprofit media guide for children's toys and media. Reviews are provided by grandparents, parents, children, teachers, librarians, writers, and artists. Parents' Choice publishes the monthly online newsletter *Parents' Choice Features.*

Video Game Voters Network
Web site: www.videogamevoters.org

The Video Game Voters Network works to organize gamers against threats to video games. The group provides news on video game legislation, encourages its members to register to vote, and suggests ways for members to take action.

Women in Games International
e-mail: info@womeningamesinternational.org
Web site: www.womeningamesinternational.org

Women in Games International is a nonprofit organization founded by industry professionals dedicated to promoting the inclusion of women in the video game industry and to improving working conditions for men and women. The group sponsors events around the world to help women break into the industry, works to find ways to retain women in the industry, and provides online mentoring.

For Further Reading

Books

DeMaria, Rusel. *Reset: Changing the Way We Look at Video Games.* San Francisco: Berret-Koehler, 2007. Provides information about the positive aspects of video games and how they can be effective vehicles for personal, educational, and professional growth.

Gee, James Paul. *What Video Games Have to Teach Us About Learning and Literacy.* New York: Palgrave Macmillan, 2007. Gee looks at how video games can be beneficial to learning.

Kafai, Yasmin B., et al. *Beyond Barbie and Mortal Kombat: New Perspectives on Gender and Gaming.* Cambridge, MA: MIT Press, 2008. The authors gather psychologists, game designers, educators, and industry insiders to analyze gender issues in gaming.

Kushner, David. *Masters of Doom: How Two Guys Created an Empire and Transformed Pop Culture.* New York: Random House Trade Paperbacks, 2004. Kushner tells the story of John Romero and John Carmack, the young developers of the hugely popular game *Doom.*

Kutner, Lawrence, and Cheryl Olson. *Grand Theft Childhood: The Surprising Truth About Violent Video Games and What Parents Can Do.* New York: Simon & Schuster, 2008. The founders of the Harvard Medical School for Mental Health and Media take an evenhanded look at the benefits and risks of video game playing by young people.

Loguidice, Bill, and Matt Barton. *Vintage Games: An Insider Look at the History of* Grand Theft Auto, Super Mario, *and the Most Influential Games of All Time.* Burlington, MA: Focal, 2009. The authors write about the history of some of the most popular video games.

Oppenheimer, Todd. *The Flickering Mind: The False Promise of Technology in the Classroom and How Learning Can Be Saved.* New York: Random House Trade Paperbacks, 2004. Oppenheimer looks at technology in the classroom and analyzes what is working and what is not.

Taylor, T.L. *Play Between Worlds: Exploring Online Game Culture.* Cambridge, MA: MIT Press, 2009. The author immerses herself in the world of online gaming and reports her discoveries on the online gaming culture.

Van Cleave, Ryan G., and Mark Griffiths. *Unplugged: My Journey into the Dark World of Video Game Addiction.* Deerfield Beach, FL: HCI, 2010. A college professor and father describes his growing obsession with the game *World of Warcraft* and his eventual descent into video game addiction.

Internet Sources

Baker, Jesse. "For Mature Audiences Only: Video Game Ratings," National Public Radio, February 22, 2010. www.npr.org/templates/story/story.php?storyId=123971771.

Brown, Eryn. "Game-Addicted and Just Fine, Thanks," *Los Angeles Times,* July 7, 2007. www.latimes.com/news/opinion/editorials/la-ed-vidgames7jul07,0,267098.story.

Chalk, Andy. "Study: Nearly One in Ten Gamers Shows Signs of Addiction," *Escapist,* March 1, 2010. www.escapistmagazine.com/news/view/98743-Study-Nearly-One-in-Ten-Gamers-Shows-Signs-of-Addiction.

Crittenden, Danielle. "Why Your Kids Should Play More Video Games," *Huffington Post,* October 24, 2006. www.huffingtonpost.com/danielle-crittenden/why-your-kids-should-play_b_32365.html.

Fulmer, Melinda. "Wii Workouts: Best of the Games," *Los Angeles Times,* March 1, 2010. http://articles.latimes.com/2010/mar/01/health/la-he-0301-fitness-games-20100301.

Govan, Paul. "We Need More Positive Family Game Ratings," *Wired,* September 22, 2009. www.wired.com/geekdad/2009/09/we-need-more-positive-family-game-ratings.

Huget, Jennifer LaRue. "Study Links Violent Video Games to Violent Thought, Action," *Washington Post,* March 1, 2010. http://voices.washingtonpost.com/checkup/2010/03/study_shows_violent_video_game.html?wprss=checkup.

John, Tracey. "Ridiculous Life Lessons from New Girl Games," *Wired,* July 13, 2009. www.wired.com/gamelife/2009/07/games-for-tweens.

Jones, Vanessa E. "The Debate over Stereotypes in Video Games Has Become a No-Win Situation," *Boston Globe*, May 5, 2008. www.boston.com/ae/games/articles/2008/05/05/a_no_win_situation/?page=full.

Kalning, Kristin. "Readers Opinion of Girl Games Mixed," MSNBC, January 21, 2009. www.msnbc.msn.com/id/28759872/ns/technology_and_science-games.

King, Stephen. "Videogame Lunacy," *Entertainment Weekly*, April 3, 2008. www.ew.com/ew/article/0,,20188502,00.html.

Maguire, Paddy. "Compulsive Gamers 'Not Addicts,'" *BBC News,* November 25, 2008. http://news.bbc.co.uk/2/hi/technology/7746471.stm.

O'Callaghan, Tiffany. "Logged On, Checked Out . . . of Relationships?" *Time,* March 1, 2010. http://wellness.blogs.time.com/2010/03/01/logged-on-checked-out-of-relationships/.

Shreve, Jenn. "Let the Games Begin: Entertainment Meets Education," *Edutopia*, December 27, 2009. www.edutopia.org/let-games-begin.

Szalavitz, Maia. "Can Playing Video Games Improve ADHD?" MSN Health & Fitness. http://health.msn.com/health-topics/adhd/article page.aspx?cp-documentid=100227286.

Web Sites

Gamasutra (www.gamasutra.com). Gamasutra is a site for people in the video game industry but offers a good look into the field for outsiders as well. The site has timely news on the industry, blogs, and in-depth articles on gaming.

GamePolitics (www.gamepolitics.com). A Web site covering issues of gaming and politics. The site features articles, game reviews, and information on legislation affecting gamers and the game industry.

GameSetWatch (www.gamesetwatch.com). GameSetWatch has exclusive columns on video games and features articles, interviews, and news from the Gamasutra Network.

Video Game Revolution (www.pbs.org/kcts/videogamerevolution/ index.html). An accompaniment to the PBS program *The Video Game Revolution,* this site is loaded with features, including playable retro arcade games, a list of the best and worst games of all time, an interactive timeline on video games, and classic game cheats.

WomenGamers (http://womengamers.com). WomenGamers offers a look at gaming from an "informed, socially-conscious, female-centered perspective." The site includes articles and a job board for careers in the gaming industry.

Index